Reclaiming Patterns of Pastoral Ministry:

Jesus and Paul

Jonathan F. Grothe

Publishing House
St. Louis

Copyright © 1988 Concordia Publishing House
3558 S. Jefferson Avenue, St. Louis, MO 63118-3968
Manufactured in the United States of America

Library of Congress Cataloging-in-Publication Data

Grothe, Jonathan F., 1941-
    Reclaiming patterns of pastoral ministry: Jesus and Paul/
Jonathan F. Grothe.
        p.   cm.
    Bibliography: p.
    ISBN 0-570-04495-2
    1. Lutheran Church—Missouri Synod—Clergy. 2. Lutheran Church—Clergy.
    3. Clergy—Office. 4. Pastoral theology—Lutheran Church.
    I. Title.
    BX8071.G76 1988
    262'.1441—dc19   87-37385

1 2 3 4 5 6 7 8 9 10   97 96 95 94 93 92 91 90 89 88

Contents

List of Abbreviations

1. Ancient Documents

Apoc. Bar (2 Bar.): The (Syriac) Apocalypse of Baruch
Ber.: Tractate Berakoth of the Mishna and Babylonian Talmud
San.: Tractate Sanhedrin of the Mishna and Babylonian Talmud
1QH: Hodayoth (Psalm), from the first cave at Qumran

2. Versions of Scripture

AAT: *The Holy Bible*, An American Translation, by W. F. Beck.
JB: The Jerusalem Bible
KJV: *The Holy Bible*, Authorized King James Version.
LXX: *Septuaginta*, ed. A. Rahlfs.
NEB: The New English Bible
RSV: *The Holy Bible*, Revised Standard Version.

3. Modern Works

BAGD: Walter Bauer, *A Greek-English Lexicon of the New Testament and Other Early Christian Literature*, trans. W. F. Arndt and F. W. Gingrich, 2d ed., rev. and augmented by F. W. Gingrich and F. W. Danker from W. Bauer's 5th ed., 1958 (Chicago: University of Chicago Press, 1979).

BDB: F. Brown, S. Driver, and C. Briggs, *A Hebrew and English Lexicon of the Old Testament* (Oxford: Clarendon, 1952).

BDF: F. Blass and A. Debrunner, *A Greek Grammar of the New Testament and Other Early Christian Literature*, a trans. and rev. of the 9th-10th German ed., incorporating supplementary notes of A. Debrunner, by R. W. Funk (Chicago: University of Chicago Press, 1961).

5

CW: James Charlesworth, ed., *The Old Testament Pseudepigrapha*, 2 vols. (Garden City: Doubleday, 1983).

ICC: The International Critical Commentary (Edinburgh: T. & T. Clark).

KEK: Kritisch-exegetischer Kommentar über das Neue Testament (Göttingen: Vandenhoeck & Ruprecht).

SB: Hermann Strack and Paul Billerbeck, *Kommentar zum Neuen Testament aus Talmud und Midrasch*, 2d ed. (Munich: Beck, 1954).

TDNT: G. Kittel, ed., *Theological Dictionary of the New Testament*, trans. and ed. by G. W. Bromiley (Grand Rapids: Eerdmans, 1964).

WA: *Dr. Martin Luthers Werke, Kritisch Gesammtausgabe* (Weimar: Herman Böhlau, 1883).

4. Other Abbreviations

k.t.l.: *kai ta loipa,* and the rest

s.v.: *sub voce,* under the lexicographical entry for the appropriate word

z. St.: *zur Stelle,* at the appropriate place (in a commentary) where the passage is discussed

Preface

This book is about the ministry. It is appropriate that those who are set aside for the office of the holy ministry read it, as well as those who aspire so to be set aside. But it is also meant for laypersons. They may not only learn from it some good things for their daily living as Christians, but they may also benefit from recognizing some of the characteristics that should be prominent in the lives and work of those who serve in the ministry. They may then encourage (or allow) their ministers to concentrate on matters truly important for the ministry, rather than allowing (or encouraging) them to be carried away by human ambition or sociological fad.

The study of Scripture and observation of the current religious scene in the United States have led to the writing of these things. Many—and they know who they are—have played a role in the experiences that have led me to the views expressed here. Needless to say, however, I myself take responsibility for the final form of these thoughts. I also hope that they may be a benefit to you, whether you serve in the office of the holy ministry, or whether you receive, support, and encourage the service of one so set aside.

In many ways, the message of this book is "all of one piece." But I could not say everything all at once. Therefore an order, of sorts, has been followed. Nevertheless, a certain degree of overlapping and cross-referencing remains. I have used endnotes not only to cite sources, but also to make important points that would otherwise have interrupted the flow of thought in the text.

Translation of Scripture, unless otherwise noted, is my own. However, when the phrase is very short, I have not tried to acknowledge a translation that duplicates the given rendering.

Acknowledgments

Parents, pastors, professors, peers, and parishioners share in this, that to them I owe a debt of gratitude for their care, instruction, guidance, advice, and patience as I learned the things reflected in these pages.

Friends and, above all, family have been helpful and understanding as I have gone through what one must go through to get thoughts down on paper in understandable form. I thank them all.

Chapter 1

Seeking Patterns
of Ministry

A. The Present State

There is an old joke in which the call committee of a congregation has before it something like the following as a characterization of a candidate for pastor:

> Age: approximately 50
> Marital Status: single or separated (details unknown)
> Formal Education: unaccredited instruction from a Jewish teacher
> Previous Service: early career unknown; recently a member of a (constantly changing) team of traveling evangelists, with longest stay in any single place approximately three years
> Comments:
> frequently in trouble with civil and religious authorities;
> claims to have received visions;
> has criticized the behavior of church leaders in public;
> preaches long sermons.

The description, of course, is of the apostle Paul, and the joke is that Paul might not have much of a chance of being called to be the pastor of a modern-day congregation. It is a measure of the degree to which we have domesticated and institutionalized the ministry that we must today look past so much accumulation of acculturated expectations in order to get back to the remarkable ministry of one such as Paul.

Modern models of ministry abound. There are various expectations of what pastors are and/or do.[1] Characterizations range from the (ontologically altered) *person* of the priest to all those things (functions, regardless of substance) that can be subsumed under "communicator" and "facilitator" (teacher, salesman, agent of social change, administrator).

It is probably not exactly what Paul meant when he spoke of "fightings without, fears within" (2 Cor. 7:5), but this variety of models and expectations is the source of considerable tension within the church (using the term broadly). Within a denomination there may be intense discussion of just what is needed to equip men for ministry, and a calling congregation may likewise agonize at length over its description of what it is looking for in a pastor. There is often a tension between what a congregation wants in a pastor and what it gets—a tension leading too often to scandalous resolutions.[2] The pull of these varying expectations may also cause tension ("lack of clarity in role definition"?) within the pastor himself, adding personal frustration to his burdens. There is always the tension between what the pastor *is* (as simultaneously a saint and a sinner) and what he *should be* and (in his heart of hearts, as a saint) *wants to be* as a pastor.[3]

It surely sounds as though things have gotten into quite a mess. It is no wonder that observers note an increasing rate of "burnout and bailout" and a decreasing number of "preacher's kids" planning to study for the ministry. The human "satisfaction level" seems not to be very high among pastors. Frustration is rampant.

What to do about it?

B. *Ad Fontes:* Back to Basics

During a recent world series, Joe Garagiola relayed to us the Willie Mays philosophy of baseball: "When they hit it, we catch it; when they throw it, we hit it." Vince Lombardi was famous for coaching (and winning) with the conviction that football boils down to blocking and tackling. The losing team practices trick plays in vain; if things are not going well, get back to basics, down to fundamentals.

Sociological surveys, ecclesiastical commissions, screening and evaluation processes and local support networks (for "reciprocal responsibility and affirmation") are all useless without a firm grasp of the fundamentals, a clear vision of reality. Clarity of vision comes only from the Light of the world and the Word that is a lamp unto our feet. Communication, evaluation, facilitation, and support are all necessary; but they are meaningless without content, criteria, purpose, and substance. We need first to listen to the Word of God, to return to the sources, to begin at the beginning.

First and foremost, the Word of God provides us with a message of comfort and assurance about the church and the ministry—and this word of comfort is intended to stand at the head of every paragraph of this effort to portray paradigms of ministry. The church is God's assembly of God's people in God's victorious Son, Jesus Christ. Our human eyes may see an all too human and worldly muddle of people and organizations on the brink of bankruptcy (financial, moral, or theological). But the "real" church is (as Luther says a seven-year-old child knows) "holy believers and sheep who hear the voice of their Shepherd."[4] The gates of hell shall not prevail against it—and neither shall red ink nor human chicanery.

The ministry, also, is a divine institution: an *office*.[5] It is the instituted office that administers the means of grace, Word and sacraments, the channels of the working of the divine power in this world. God's Word does not return to Him void (Is. 55:11). His power in Baptism and His presence in Holy Communion are not dependent on the personal faith nor on the orthodoxy of the human servant who administers them.[6] Human weaknesses and the various frustrations connected with service in the ministry do not nullify the power of God. Scripture assures us that God's love is in us and that He who is in us is greater than he who is in the world (1 John 4:4). There is no need for despair over grace and salvation because of the tensions in and about the ministry.

A clear vision of the ministry *is* a serious matter for the health of God's people and for the spread of His reign among all people. Not the efficacy of His Word but the effectiveness of our bearing witness to the Gospel is at stake. One's vision of reality affects valuation, and values motivate behavior, and the words and deeds of those who serve in the ministry are means by which God conducts *His* ministry, invading the world of time and space with His eternal Word.

In addition to this word of comfort about the divine initiative and control, Scripture provides us with information about the ministry and the conduct of those who serve in it. The following pages attempt to extract from Scripture some of this information and to contribute to a clearer vision of what is involved in the ministry. Perhaps this refocusing on some fundamentals may ameliorate some of the feelings of tension and frustration.

This attempt is not undertaken as a systematization of the content of prescriptive passages about the ministry in Scripture.[7] Nor is it a rehearsal of Paul's career, an evaluation of each of his letters, or an exposition of his doctrine. It concentrates, rather, on passages which reveal Paul in action *in* the ministry. Hovering over the apostle at work, it seeks to delineate lines that run through the whole of his ministry and to find the ways in which they connect to the rest of Scripture. This book aims to reclaim patterns of ministry by examining especially the model provided by the apostle who wrote: "Become imitators of me, even as I myself also am of Christ" (1 Cor. 11:1).

C. Jesus, Paul, and Other Ministers

These words of Paul, in their context, have a special application, which shall be expounded below, when they serve as the theme for a later chapter. But in addition to whatever else they may say, Paul's words in 1 Corinthians 11:1 suggest a chain: Jesus—Paul—us. It is a chain of imitation and representation, a chain of responsibility and authority. Herein lies the rationale of this book: in Paul can be seen patterns of the ministry of Jesus, and these should be paradigmatic for us.

The idea of this "chain of ministry" has been worked on in a book by Colin Kruse, a New Testament professor from Australia.[8] He delineates, helpfully, three lines of continuity extending from Jesus to Paul: "apostle," "servant," and "bearer of the Spirit."[9]

Apostle

There is, in fact, a chain of representation and imitation which comes to expression in the word "apostle." Jesus, above all, is *the* apostle (Heb. 3:1). He is the *one sent* from God to reveal God. Whoever sees Him sees God (John 14:9), and whoever hears Him hears Him who sent Him (John 15:15; cf. Luke 10:16). He is, in fact, the Son of

God Himself, sent into the world to tabernacle among men and make the Father known (John 1:14, 18). Jesus' self-consciousness is the origin of this kind of talk, but it may be appropriate to note the similarity of it to what is expressed in the Jewish legal institution of the *shaliach*: "the one sent by a man is as the man himself."[10] The Son is one with the Father and so "represents" Him perfectly. He is the perfect image and "imitator" of God.

The designation of the twelve and (after Easter) others, including Paul, as apostles fits right in with this pattern of representation and imitation, authority and responsibility. During Jesus' lifetime, the twelve were especially commissioned to extend His work through their persons (Matt. 10:1–42). They were His agents, His representatives; through them He worked and whoever heeded them heeded Him. Paul's apostleship, likewise, was no matter of human arrangement; he was on a par with those others who had been specially and directly called and set aside by Jesus to be extensions of His presence and His power.[11]

Those who serve in the ministry today are not on a par with the twelve, eyewitnesses of the events that are the genesis of the Gospel and the foundation-layer of the building of the church. Nor are they "apostles" in the sense of Paul, directly called and commissioned by the risen Lord. Those who serve in the ministry today are *normed by* the apostolic testimony and are called *mediately* by God *through* the church. But they serve in the ministry that originated with Jesus (the One sent from God), was continued by Him through His apostles, and has been preserved in the church ever since. As successors of the apostles, those who serve today are similarly set aside to be stewards of the mysteries of God and are sent to proclaim His Word to all the world. Their ministry is "Christian" and "apostolic"; they are called to represent the One sent from God and to imitate Paul, even as he imitates Christ.

Servant

The Christ whose imitation Paul commends defined His mission in terms of the Suffering Servant. Colin Kruse rightly also features "servanthood" as an element of continuity in the ministry of Christ and that of Paul. While acknowledging the titles "Son of God" and "Messiah" and using for Himself the (deliberately?) ambiguous "Son of Man," Jesus nowhere more eloquently described His mission than in the famous logion of Mark 10:45, which summarizes the mission of the Suffering Servant: "For also the Son of Man did not come to be ministered to but rather to minister and to give His life a ransom in place of many." The stamp of the Servant, the Righteous One who suffers vicariously on the cross, is on all that we know of Jesus' ministry.[12]

Paul likewise regularly characterized himself as a servant of Christ (δοῦλος Χριστοῦ, next to apostle, Rom. 1:1) and understood the "imitation" of Jesus to include a participation in Jesus' sufferings. A slave (δοῦλος) is not his own person; he does his master's will. He is nothing; his master is everything. Like the Old Testament prophets, the apostle Paul both humbles himself and magnifies his office when he calls himself Christ's servant.[13] Boasting of one's own achievements is ruled out; proper pride and joy is in the Lord and in the sufferings that come upon one who belongs to Christ, the Crucified. As the apostle of the Crucified, Paul's servanthood includes his personal weaknesses (of which he boasts, 2 Cor. 11:21–12:10) and his sufferings, which he connects to Christ's (Col. 1:24–26; cf. Gal. 6:17). Such a conformity to the servanthood of the Crucified One is part also of the servant model to be continued by those who now serve Christ in the ministry.

It is appropriate to search in Scripture for the patterns of Christ's ministry revealed in Paul. With Jesus it all began, and from Jesus it all proceeds. He Himself said: "Follow me! . . . Take My yoke upon you and learn from Me, for I am meek and humble in heart" (Matt. 9:9; 11:29). In Paul we have a reflection of Jesus, a mirroring of His ministry, a pattern portrayed in a number of paradigms. This book delineates some of those paradigms.

Spirit

Certainly, from Jesus to Paul and all the apostles there goes more than just a pattern and a command to imitate. More than human determination to imitate is needed. Jesus is also bearer of the Spirit and dispenser of the Spirit. On Easter evening Jesus said, "Even as the Father has sent Me, I also am sending you" (John 20:21). He then breathed His Spirit into the apostles, thus instituting the ministry and establishing the means to continue the bringing of the

14

Word of life to the world. Paul is an imitator of Christ because he is a recipient of and a bearer of the Spirit. The Spirit of God is the assurance that the ministry is God's institution through which God's power is at work. Only by the Spirit of God can the ministry in the church today imitate Paul and so imitate Christ.

This book examines some specific incidents and relationships in Paul's ministry and the things he wrote about them. From them it aims to delineate some specific patterns of apostolic service and paradigms for ministry today. Building upon the basis laid in this chapter, each subsequent chapter will focus on one such "pattern," sketching the language throughout the Bible that reflects the picture, and briefly describing both how the ministry of Jesus fulfilled the picture and how all the apostles continued in the same pattern. The heart of each chapter, however, will be an examination of those passages that reveal Paul recapitulating the pattern of relationship, in word and in deed, and thereby leaving us an example to emulate.

To emulate his example is by no means easy. The author knows all too well how often he has failed to follow these paradigms. They are hard. They are, in fact, humanly impossible. But from Jesus to Paul to the ministry in the church there flows not only a pattern, but also a power. It is the power of the Holy Spirit who teaches the pattern, bestows authority and responsibility, and fills human beings—called servants and "earthen vessels"—with power. And so men carry out God's work and continue Jesus' ministry in the holy ministry. Difficult? Yes. Impossible? With God all things are possible.

Chapter 2

Parent and Child

A. The Biblical Language of Life

Thy Word meant LIFE, triumphant, hurled
Through every cranny of Thy world . . . .[1]

God's Word creates; it creates LIFE. In the beginning God said: "Let there be . . . ." And there was. God breathed into the man the breath of life and the man became a living being (Gen. 2:7), "the son of God" (Luke 3:38). The consequences of sin were described in the words of threat: "Thou shalt surely die" (Gen. 2:17). But the gracious promise held out hope for the triumph of human life by the power of God's Word when Eve's Seed, *the* Son of God, shall have crushed the head of the death-dealing enemy (Gen. 3:15).

All that follows in the Old Testament and the New reiterates this connection and this promise and tells what God undertook to do in order to fulfill it. The psalmist confessed: "For with Thee is the fountain of life" (Ps. 36:9, RSV), and Job (10:12) says: "Life and steadfast love Thou hast appointed for me, and Thy visitation hath guarded my spirit." In the offer of His gracious plan of salvation God confronted people, saying, "I have set before you life and death, blessing and curse; therefore choose life, that you and your descendants may live, loving the Lord your God, obeying His voice, and cleaving to Him; for that means life to you and length of days . . . . " (Deut. 30:19–20, RSV)[2] He continued to hold out to them the promise: "I will put my Spirit within you, and you shall live" (Ezek. 37:14, RSV).

One expression of this promise of life was in the language of a parent-child relationship. The Chosen One of the promise is "my first-born son" (Ex. 4:22), and the indictment of the people of Israel is based on the fact that "sons have I made strong and great" (Is.

16

1:2). Of Him through whom all would be made alive it is said: "I shall be to Him Father and He shall be to me Son" (2 Sam. 7:14), and: "My Son art Thou, I this day have begotten Thee" (Ps. 2:7).[3]

He toward whom all these words of promise pointed, the Word Incarnate, the Second Adam, the true Israel, was born by the power of the Holy Spirit of the virgin Mary. He was attested, in truth, as the Son of God, the One in whom is God's life, who enjoys communion with His Father in a unity of being, a unity of will, and a unity in love. During His earthly ministry He raised men from the dead as a sign of the power that was in Him and said: "I am the resurrection and the life" (John 11:25), and "I came in order that they might have life, indeed, that they might have it abundantly" (John 10:10). His apostles, moreover, testified: "In Him was life" (John 1:4), "who took away the power of death and caused life and immortality to shine through the Gospel" (2 Tim. 1:10). The Word of the Gospel of Jesus Christ, which those apostles spoke and which we speak is, therefore, "the word of life" (1 John 1:1).

Scripture describes what happens to an individual whom God saves in Jesus Christ as "being begotten" and "being born." The passages that come to mind most quickly are, again, in the Gospel According to St. John, where the prolog says (1:12–13): "But as many as received Him, He gave to them the right to become children ($\tau\acute{\epsilon}\kappa\nu\alpha$) of God, to those believing in His name, who were begotten not by blood nor by will of flesh nor by will of man, but rather by God." In the famous conversation with Nicodemus, Jesus says (John 3:3): "Truly, truly, I say to you, unless a person is begotten/born anew/from above, he is not able to see the reign of God."

The other apostles reflect the same thought. James says (1:18, RSV): "Of His own will He brought us forth ($\dot{\alpha}\pi\epsilon\kappa\acute{\upsilon}\eta\sigma\epsilon\nu$) by the word of truth . . . ." St. Paul in Titus 3:5 speaks of God's saving us "in virtue of His own mercy, by the washing of regeneration ($\delta\iota\dot{\alpha}$ $\lambda o\upsilon\tau\rho o\hat{\upsilon}$ $\pi\alpha\lambda\iota\gamma\gamma\epsilon\nu\epsilon\sigma\acute{\iota}\alpha\varsigma$) and renewal in the Holy Spirit . . . " (RSV). People formerly dead in trespasses and sins have "been brought from death to life" (Rom. 6:13) through the power of the Spirit of God, the Spirit of sonship (Rom. 8:15). The one who is in a right relationship to God by faith shall *live* (Gal. 3:11; cf. Rom. 1:17) and, with the Spirit of God's Son in his heart, he calls God "Abba," "Father" (Gal. 4:6; cf. Rom. 8:15).

In and of themselves these are no startling observations. On the

17

basis of such Biblical language, every baptized, believing Christian rightly claims to have been "born again." But that rebirth is a miracle, even as the sustaining of that new spiritual life is by the Spirit's power. (We are more "kept in the faith" than "keeping the faith." The anthropocentric, "born-again" religiosity popular in the United States must be rejected.)

B. Pauline Corollaries

Striking, however, and less than fully appreciated, is the way in which St. Paul uses this same thought to create expressions that refer to the special relationship between himself and "his" converts. *He* is their "father" or "mother," and they are *his* "children." This vision of their relationship lies beneath many of the things written in Paul's letters; it is even a part of the very rationale for his writing most of them. The letters are extensions of his "apostolic presence"[4] to (in most cases) "his" churches. The thought comes to explicit expression in several specific passages, to which we now turn our attention.

1. 1 Corinthians 4:14–15

> I am writing these things to you not causing you to turn away in shame but rather admonishing my beloved children. For even if you have thousands of teachers, nevertheless you do not have many fathers: for in Christ Jesus, through the Gospel, I myself begot you.

The context of this passage, of course, is Paul's response to news of disturbing developments in doctrine and behavior among the Christians in his "brilliant and wayward child,"[5] the congregation at Corinth. Paul is admonishing them to return to and remain in the Gospel that he had delivered to them and thus to be "imitators" of him, "good and faithful" children "in the Lord."[6] To reinforce that appeal, Paul plans to send to them Timothy, his "good and faithful child (τέκνον)" (v. 17), a convert from his missionary work who had been specially chosen by Paul (Acts 16:1–3) and who served in the Gospel with Paul "as a child (τέκνον) with a father" (Phil. 2:22).

Paul's remarkable expression here remains carefully consistent with the Biblical language introduced above. God is the source of this new life in Christ through the powerful word of the Gospel. Paul guards carefully against any misunderstanding. He desires not to have sons in the image of and for the glory of Paul, but in the image of *Christ*, who dwells in him and whose servant and apostle he is.

This emphasis is especially significant; it is related to Paul's combat against factionalism in Corinth:

> For whenever someone might say: 'I am Paul's,' but another person: 'I am Apollos,' are you not [all] human beings? What, then, is Apollos? What is Paul? Servants through whom you believed, indeed, to each one as the Lord granted. I planted, Apollos watered, but God caused growth. (1 Cor. 3:4–7)

These words make it clear again that the *power* of this begetting to life and growth in life is not from Paul but rather is from God through His servants (διάκονοι). Whatever special relationships there may be, they may by no means become causes for pride or factionalism within God's one family.

Considering the presence of factionalism, it is surprising that in 1 Corinthians 4:14–15 Paul *does* claim an exclusive relationship to these Corinthian Christians. They are *his* children and, though (in contrast to faithful Timothy) they are wayward, they merit and should heed *his* admonition. He, Paul, alone (in contradistinction to the many "teachers")[7] is their father; he *himself* (ἐγώ, emphatic, not another) begot them.

How has this come to be? To effect the "new birth" of conversion and salvation, there has been established the ministry of the Gospel, the external means of grace, namely: the preaching of the Word and the administration of the sacraments. This is expressed, for example, in Romans 10:14–15, where Paul comments on Joel 2:32 (quoted in Rom. 10:13): "Every one who calls upon the name of the Lord will be saved" (RSV). By means of a series of rhetorical questions, Paul explains the need for the ministry of the means of grace and for men to serve in it: "How, then, might they call upon Him in whom they have not believed? How might they believe in Him of whom they have not heard? How might they hear without one who preaches? How might they preach unless they be sent?" Paul was such a sent preacher, an apostle, an earthen vessel (2 Cor. 4:7) bearing the treasure of the Gospel's ministry to the Corinthians.

He thus appropriately refers to *himself* as their father, who begot them. Every human father is nothing but a created, cooperating agent of God the Creator. In the "miracle" of procreation, the human father participates as an agent for the planting of the seed. But he is unable to "make life" (cause conception) apart from the divine power of the Creator Himself. So also Paul, as the preaching apostle, was a called, sent, privileged, cooperating, minor (but, in God's plan, necessary) partner with (or, better, servant of) God. Through his preaching and baptizing[8] he begot and God created new spiritual life in those who came to faith. He and only he was their "father" in this special sense. It does not mean that he owned them (any more than a parent owns a child) or that he could tyrannize or abuse them. But there was between them and him a relationship unlike that between them and anyone else. It was a relationship of care, responsibility, obedience, and even including, as the case may be, feelings of frustration, shame, or pride.[9] It is all that is involved in the relationship of parent and child.

2. Philemon 10

Paul uses the same expression in Philemon 10. Philemon's runaway slave has come to Paul in prison.[10] Paul writes to Philemon (and to Apphia, Archippus, and the "church in your house," Philemon 1–2) in order to effect a reconciliation.[11] Artfully avoiding the mention of the renegade's name until he has recounted the recovery of this lost person's *real* life, Paul writes: "I beseech you concerning[12] my child (τέκνου), whom I begot in these chains, Onesimus" (v. 10).

This is no mere picture of the elderly Paul taking the young slave "under his wing," as an ersatz parent. Rather, what has happened is that Onesimus has been converted: he has become a Christian. This is clear from the wording of verses 15 and 16, where Paul tells Philemon that Onesimus "was separated [from you] temporarily in order that you might receive him eternally, *no longer* as [just] a slave but as more than a slave, as a beloved brother [in Christ]." "In the Lord" Onesimus is now Philemon's *brother*, and Paul's *child*.

Although "brother" can be used broadly of all who are in Christ regardless of who preached to them, it is probably correct to say that Philemon, too, is counted as Paul's "child" (or perhaps "grandchild") in Christ. A resident of Colossae (cf. Col. 4:9), Philemon most likely had never met Paul (cf. Col. 2:1); but he was probably con-verted to Christianity through the evangelizing work of Epaphras (Col. 1:7), a mission undertaken under Paul's aegis during his min-istry in Ephesus (see Acts 19:10). Thus a special bond of life and responsibility, love and respect existed also between Paul and Phi-lemon. Paul refers to this in Philemon 8 and 9: "Therefore, although having great boldness in Christ to order you [to do] that which is required, I appeal, rather, on the basis of love." Again in verse 19 Paul mentions what he claims he need not refer to: " . . . that I might not [have to] say to you that you owe to me your very life."[13]

This use of father-child language is not unique to Paul and Chris-tianity. "Life" is a code word for salvation in other ancient religions, and the agents who administer that which gives salvation/life are also sometimes described as the fathers of the individuals so bene-fited. This is apparent in Judaism, where the teacher (rabbi) can be called the father of the student whom he has instructed in the Torah.[14] We might well consider this usage to have grown out of the context of liturgical (Ex. 12:24–27), ethical (Deut. 4:9), and prac-tical (Prov. 1:8) instruction from fathers to sons testified to in the Old Testament. The human practice might be the basis for the re-ligious usage. Inherent in the transfer is the assumption that the material taught creates life. Students of ancient religions have also found evidence of a similar usage outside of the Biblical tradition (although, in some cases, the Christian tradition may have influenced the groups in question). Some post-New Testament documents call the mystagogue (ὁ μύων) in the mystery religions the father of the one initiated into the mystery (ὁ μυόμενος).[15] Once again, the as-sumption is that the initiation is a bringing to life—salvation.

This has led to the suggestion that Paul is just repeating a con-ventional figure of speech.[16] It is tempting, at this point, to agree at least that Paul is using language metaphorically. Desiring to describe spiritual realities about spiritual relationships, Paul might refer to a relationship that is common to human experience. In the technical terms regarding the use of comparisons in language,[17] the immediate human experience of the relationship of a "literal" father and son would be the *vehicle* and the spiritual level of the relationship of God, the apostle and his converts, would be the *tenor*, to which the significance in the point(s) of comparison would be transferred.

This may be an apt description from the point of view of a

dispassionate analyst of the the use of language. But the believing reader of Scripture sees evidence that Paul believed otherwise. Paul does not, in fact, move inductively from the human, physical ("literal") relationship to the spiritual; rather, in Ephesians 3:14–15 he asserts that the real picture of the relationship is just the opposite: "For this reason I bow my knees before the Father, from whom every fatherhood in heaven and on earth is named . . . ."

Prior to all experience is God, the Creator, the Father, the source of all life. Deduced from that fatherhood of God is every other "patria," clan, or nation descended from or named after a father. Deductively, from the point of view of faith, it is the relationships originating in God that are prior, and the human relationships are derived.[18]

If we are to appreciate these passages of St. Paul, we must recognize that for him the life-giving fatherhood of God is that which is primary and real and which, therefore, gives substance and meaning to the word "father." That is the word's true referent and therefore its "literal" meaning. The use of the concept to describe human relationships is secondary, derived, by way of comparison, and therefore "metaphorical."

This means that while the application of the word "father" to Paul in relationship to the Corinthians and Onesimus is still metaphorical, its use in this religious sphere actually takes us closer to the spiritual realities in which (for Paul) the heart of the meaning of the word lies. It is, then, more than a "manner of speaking," more than a "parable," more than a "picture."[19] Its use in this context opens a window onto the mysterious reality of God and the way in which the power of God in the Gospel works in and through the earthen vessels who are the ordained servants in the ministry.[20]

3. Galatians 4:19

This understanding is corroborated by Paul's stark use of language in Galatians 4:19. This is no canned metaphor, but the expression of the same mystery in a different mode: the birth pangs of motherhood. With all the deep personal involvement of an anxious, suffering mother, Paul closes his most personal appeal to the Galatians with these words in Gal. 4:19–20: "My children (τέκνα), whom I am again giving birth to amid throes until Christ be formed in you.

But I could wish to be present with you now and to change the tone of my voice, for I am perplexed about you."

The "children" designation recurs here. The Galatians are Paul's converts, his special concern and responsibility. But now Paul, though male, expresses his agency in their new birth through the use of the word ὠδίνω: "I suffer birth pangs," or "I bear amid throes."[21] The physical and personal involvement, the work, the "pain" and the "suffering" of a mother as God's privileged and chosen cooperating agent in the miraculous life-creating process of birth, is an expression—perhaps a stronger one than "I begot"—of the unparalleled closeness and intense involvement of the apostle in the new birth of his converts.

The phrase "until Christ be formed in you" is capable of several interpretations (justification, sanctification, eschatological completion). But the passive form of the verb makes it clear that this is the work of God the Holy Spirit *in* Paul, not of "mother" Paul himself. As a tentative explanation, it might refer to the time before one arrives at the point when he is a ("viable") Christian believer, trusting in the pure Gospel. On this reading, the reference would be to the Galatians' conversion, their coming to faith in the pure Gospel, rather than to their sanctification process, their progress toward the goal of "the full stature of manhood in Christ" (Eph. 4:13), or to their eschatological perfection, their becoming completely conformed to the image of Christ (Phil. 1:6; Rom. 8:29). This explanation fits best with the situation addressed in Galatians, in which Paul is concerned about his hearers' saving faith in the pure Gospel, unalloyed (and so unpolluted and not destroyed) by the addition of works of law. If the Galatians have that trust in the pure Gospel, then they have been "born," and Christ dwells within them. The subsequent growth and strength, the maturation to full manhood and eschatological perfection may come.

The debate over the specific meaning of the phrase notwithstanding, the passage surely expresses the depth and the intensity of Paul's personal involvement in and responsibility for the spiritual birth and life of his converts. He is, spiritually, their "mother" as well as their father.

4. 1 Thessalonians 2:7–8

Similar language recurs in this admittedly difficult passage. In an emotion-charged letter to his recent converts, Paul writes:

... but we became gentle[22] in your midst, as when a nursing mother might warmly embrace her own children; being thus tenderly affectionate toward you, we were well disposed to impart to you not only the Gospel of God but even our very own lives, for you became beloved to us.

While the expression is cast as a simile and not a stark metaphor, the words here express the appropriateness of the mother-child relationship as a model for understanding the relationship of apostle and converts. "Nurse" (τροφός) may mean a "wet-nurse" as a substitute for the actual mother, but it may also mean "a mother while nursing."[23] The latter is the case here, as is made clear by the reference to *her own (ἑαυτῆς)*" children. "Warmly embrace" (θάλπῃ) means "cherish" in a secondary sense (Eph. 5:29), but it is the warming incubation of the mother bird in Deuteronomy 22:6 (LXX), that which God has made the ostrich to forget (Job 39:13–18, LXX). It is a mother-nurture word. "Being tenderly affectionate" (ὁμειρόμενοι) is a rare and difficult word, which cannot be shown to be used in any specifically mother-child contexts. But the translation above: "impart to you ... even our very own lives" (RSV: "share with you ... our own selves") brings out the possible "birth-nurture" implications in the Greek phrase: μεταδοῦναι ὑμῖν ... καὶ τὰς ἑαυτῶν ψυχάς. Thus several expressions in these verses, too, suggest strongly that Paul envisioned the relationship between himself and his converts to be that of a mother and child.[24]

The communion of saints is a perfect and complete union with God and with each other in Christ. Hence, while personal relationships from our lives on this earth will not be forgotten in the life of the world to come, their distinctiveness will pale into insignificance when we "know as we are known" and "God is all and in all." In heaven they neither marry nor are given in marriage; one family in Christ, all are closer to each other than even to spouse. Furthermore, Jesus said: "He who does the will of God" (which is to believe in Him whom God has sent) "is my brother and sister and mother" (Mark 3:35; cf. John 6:29). Unity in Christ, realized in heaven, transcends such relationships as we must count as important now.

C. The Ministry as Parenthood

But such relationships are important now. What was true of Paul as a bearer of the ministry of the Gospel is true also of all who follow in his train in the "prophetic and apostolic" ministry. They are personal agents for the creation and sustenance of spiritual life: spiritual parents. While "pastor" is the more common title among most Protestants to express the caring, nurturing, and leading responsibilities of the ministry,[25] "father," properly understood, is also as appropriate. It must not become a title of exaltation or personal authority by virtue of a man's human qualities, nor may it be a source of human pride or of abuse. But it is a title which expresses something true about the ministry and a proper respect for what is worked through the men set aside for the ministry. For each one of us as individual Christians has been and is dependent upon the means of grace for the spiritual birth and the sustenance of our life in Christ; and the means of grace, the Word and the sacraments, come administered by men set aside to that service.

The ministry is the treasure; the men set aside for it are the earthen vessels. Because of what is wrought through them, they are rightly called agents of the life-creating power, "mothers" and "fathers" in Christ. The Holy Spirit does not work except through external means; therefore, this new birth does not take place apart from the cooperating ministry of the human vessels through whom the creative power is at work.

Accordingly, Martin Luther, after having treated three kinds of fatherhood (by blood, of a household, and of a nation) under the Fourth Commandment in his Large Catechism, writes:[26]

> Besides these, there are also spiritual fathers—not like those in the papacy who applied this title to themselves but performed no fatherly office. For the name spiritual father belongs only to those who govern and guide us by the Word of God. St. Paul boasts that he is a father in I Cor. 4:15, where he says, "I became your father in Christ Jesus through the Gospel." Since such persons are fathers, they are entitled to honor, even above all others.

Those who "watch over" the souls of the Christian "common people" (paragraph 161) are fathers worthy of honor, even a "double honor" (1 Tim. 5:17). Equally to be emphasized is the responsibility, a "double responsibility" of the "fatherly office" which they thus fill, "as men who shall give account" (Heb. 13:17; cf. James 3:1).

It might be helpful to distinguish, in practical application, three levels of intensity with which the "father" or "mother" idea might apply to those who now serve in the ministry:

First and most specifically would be the long-lasting personal relationship between the individual person in the ministry who evangelized, converted and/or baptized another individual. This would be the closest to the kind of relationship Paul refers to between himself and the Corinthians, the Galatians, and Onesimus.

Second would be an extended usage, in accord with which not only are the individual servants in the ministry who baptized us our "fathers," but also those from whom they heard and learned the Gospel are reckoned as our spiritual ancestors. Thus, longitudinally, we rightly claim such as Luther and Augustine as fathers or "grandfathers" in the faith, even as Paul (through Epaphras) was a source of spiritual life to Philemon and others who had not seen his face (Col. 2:1).

Most general would be a usage in which all who are "born again" through the means of grace express their awareness of their dependence, in their spiritual life, on the ministry by extending the application of the concept to all who serve in the ministry. This generalizing, of course, loses precisely the close human connection claimed and treasured by St. Paul in 1 Corinthians 4 and Galatians 4, but it does gain a breadth that can have a good effect on the vision of the relationship between any given pastor and his congregation. Any individual who is administering the means of grace in the office of the ministry is serving in a calling that is like that of a parent: the life of every Christian in his care depends on him.

D. Consequences

When God calls and sets aside a man to be a pastor, that man becomes a necessary cooperating human vessel for the power of God to create and sustain life in others through the means of grace. Ordination does not effect a change-of-essence nor bestow on the candidate an indelible character, but it does signify a high calling to become a steward of the mysteries of God—life-giving mysteries. The calling into this "spiritual parenthood" may not become a basis for human pride nor a demand for personal privilege.[27] The authority of the ministry is a right and a responsibility. It is nothing else than, and extends no farther than, the authority of the Holy Spirit in the Word.

This vision of the ministry as parenthood, rooted in Paul's practice and words, may lead to some helpful consequences as pastors and laity evaluate their relationship and allow their behavior to be reshaped accordingly. It means that each pastor should recognize his dependence, as a Christian person, on the means of grace for his own spiritual life and health. Correspondingly, he should be able to see that the power of his ministry is not his, but God's. Those who will be "indispensable," or their own boss, will get it all wrong. The ministry is a trust, a partnership with the Creator, like parenthood. Those brought to spiritual life are *God's* children, entrusted to spiritual care, just like children in their parents' care.

It also means a relationship of love and respect in which failings and shortcomings are not parlayed into resentment, rebellion, and "firings" of the pastor. Pastors, like human parents, make errors in judgment or overlook, at times, some important need, due to their own limitations. Children who are loved, and who know they are loved, learn to accept such failings in their parents, confident of the basically sound relationship of love. The pastor whose parishioners *know* of his love and care for them do not let his shortcomings plant a "root of bitterness," which grows into the tree of murmuring against appointed leaders and bears the fruit of dissension and division.[28] Where the family is well-cared for and spiritually healthy, such rancorous terminations, now all too frequent, may be averted.

It means, finally, that the ministry is no nine-to-five job. It is by no means a job; it is a calling to the full-time responsibility and joy of parenthood. Just as a parent, with a constant concern for her children, can be awakened out of a sound sleep by a child's cry in need, so also a pastor serves in a relationship characterized by constant concern for the spiritual health of the family committed to his care. A parent knows instinctively the needs of each child; the pastor applies Law and Gospel as needed in the spiritual care (*Seelsorge*) of his people.

It is not easy. "How to" courses can't teach it. No canned program does it. It calls for commitment, self-sacrifice, and parental love. A vision of the ministry in the pattern of parenthood helps to provide a sense of the kind of love and commitment involved.[29] It is the kind of sense of attachment which led Paul to have his congregations

27

constantly in his thoughts and in his prayers and to count among the sufferings that are the true marks of his apostleship also the "daily concern, the care of all the churches" (2 Cor. 11:28). But like the daily burden and never-completed work of parenthood, it is a work that is a joy and a burden that is light.

Chapter 3

The Death and the Life

A. The Biblical Pattern

As mysterious as life is, so mysterious also is death. Neither is fully within our ken. Human experience regularly observes their relationship in the order of life and death. The Word of God has more to say, presenting the order as death and life.

1. Death: Necessary, Vicarious

"In the day that thou eatest thereof thou shalt surely die" (Gen. 2:17, KJV). This is the Word of God. If He is to be true to His Word, He is bound to fulfill this threat. The wages of sin is death. Given this Word of God and the fact of sin, man's death is necessary, inevitable. The new spiritual life into which human beings may be born is a life that cannot be unless this Word of the Lord is fulfilled also: Death to the sinner!

In the woman's Seed, whose heel was bruised, this Word was fulfilled. It was God's plan from all eternity to send Jesus as a means of expiation for sin, thus showing that despite having passed over former sins in forbearance God was still "righteous," true to His word both to punish sin and to send a Savior (Rom. 3:27–28). Death was absolutely necessary; it was also accomplished vicariously, on our behalf, in Christ. He was true man, the second Adam, a representative incorporating all humanity; He died the death that man had earned.[1]

With an eye already on the fulfillment of this plan in Jesus, God instituted in the Old Testament period ceremonies that revealed the necessity of death and the vicarious nature of that death, which would having saving power. The blood of the lamb saved the people from the angel of death at the Passover, and animal sacrifices were prescribed for sin offerings and for purification on the day of atonement. (The Epistle to the Hebrews argues that these were not fully effective in and of themselves, and so must have been forward-pointing prophecies-in-action.[2]) Other incidents likewise foreshadowed the same truth: a ram took Isaac's place (Gen. 22:13); and those who looked upon the serpent "lifted up" were rescued (Num. 21:9). But the clearest prophecy in the Old Testament came in Isaiah's words describing the Suffering Servant of the Lord:

> But He was wounded for our transgressions, He was bruised for our iniquities; upon Him was the chastisement that made us whole, and with His stripes we are healed. . . . The Lord hath laid on Him the iniquity of us all. . . . Yet He bore the sin of many, and made intercession for the transgressors. (Is. 53:5, 6c, 12d, RSV)

Here is taught most clearly the necessity of death for sin and the power of the Servant's death to generate life for others, as God designates His death as saving. The Epistle to the Hebrews says that without the shedding of blood there is no forgiveness (Heb. 9:22), and:

> Since therefore the children share in flesh and blood, He Himself likewise partook of the same nature, that through death He might destroy him who has the power of death, that is, the devil, and deliver all those who through fear of death were subject to lifelong bondage. (Heb. 2:14–15, RSV)

Nowhere else are both the necessity of death because of sin and the divine solution of the saving, life-giving death of Christ more succinctly expressed than in Romans 5:19:

> For as by one man's disobedience many [= all] have been made to be placed in a category bearing the label "sinners," so by one man's obedience [Christ's obedience, including His obedience "unto death"] many will be made to be placed in the category labeled "righteous."

2. Jesus and His Mission

Jesus certainly understood His mission to be the fulfillment of this plan, namely, that a necessary vicarious death must take place in order for the birth of new life to occur. In Mark 10:45 He described what He was about in terms reminiscent of Isaiah 53: "For even the Son of Man came not to be ministered unto, but to minister, and to give His life a ransom for many." In John 10 He taught: "I am come that they might have life, and that they might have it more abundantly. I am the Good Shepherd: the Good Shepherd giveth His life for the sheep. . . . No man taketh it from Me, but I lay it down of Myself" (John 10:10b–11, 18a, KJV).

In John 12 the apostle records Jesus' explanation in the parable: "Truly, truly, I say to you, unless a grain of wheat falls into the earth and dies, it remains alone; but if it dies, it bears much fruit" (John 12:24). This was the fulfillment of God's Word promising judgment and salvation, as He explained on the road to Emmaus: " 'Was it not necessary that the Christ should suffer these things and enter into His glory?' And beginning with Moses and all the prophets, He interpreted to them in all the Scriptures the things concerning Himself" (Luke 24:26–27, RSV).

3. The Sending of the Apostles

To *all* of His followers, then, Jesus taught that this same death-and-life pattern would be the outcome of their lives. "For whosoever will save his life shall lose it; but whosoever shall lose his life for My sake and the Gospel's, the same shall save it" (Mark 8:35, KJV).

To the chosen circle of the twelve, to the apostles, who are set aside to be the special channels for the authoritative continuation of Jesus' mission, He says things that point to the *extraordinary* way in which their call into His ministry will issue in a recapitulation of this same death-life pattern for them. To the *apostles* he says, "ye shall be hated of all men for My name's sake" (Matt. 10:22, KJV; cf. vv. 1–5), for: "The disciple is not above his master, nor the servant above his lord. It is enough for the disciple that he be as his master, and the servant as his lord" (Matt. 10:24–25).[3]

Discipleship and especially apostleship are marked by a sharing in the Master's lot. The sons of thunder, James and John, wanted places of distinction as leaders (Mark 10:35–37). This was not for Jesus to grant; His call to them was to follow Him. What He *could* promise was that, as His followers, they would be "baptized with the same baptism I am baptized with" (Mark 10:39).[4] In the same

31

vein, Jesus told Peter specifically: "When you are old, you will stretch out your hands, and another will gird you and carry you where you do not wish to go" (John 21:18b, RSV). By this word, the evangelist John tells us, Jesus was showing by what death Peter would glorify God (v. 19).

What applies to James, John, and Peter applies clearly and equally to all the apostles. As *apostles* they were being sent, as representatives and imitators. So, on Easter evening, while showing them His pierced hands, feet, and side, the risen Jesus commissioned them into a ministry like His: "As the Father has sent Me,[5] so send I you" (John 20:21). Apostleship (representation and imitation), servanthood (giving up one's life for the sake of others), and ministry (*the* ministry—bestowal of the Spirit to authorize Gospel ministry) are all intertwined in this scene. Being called into the ministry of the Word of life means being set on a path that leads through death to life.

B. Life Through Death in Paul

Apostleship and servanthood and ministry, life through death, are also intertwined in the career of the apostle who was not present with those others on that first Easter evening, but who was called and commissioned later, on the road to Damascus. In that encounter Saul of Tarsus learned that a crucified Messiah was no contradiction in terms, and that the birth to new life necessarily involved a death.

1. Incorporation into Jesus' Death and Life

Scattered throughout Paul's recorded sermons and his letters lies ample testimony of his emphasis on the necessary vicarious death that gives new life. He repeated and expanded upon formulae from Jesus' own preaching and from the Christian (pre-Pauline) tradition. In Galatians he spoke of Jesus Christ, "who gave Himself for our sins to deliver us from the present evil age" (1:4), and said that by his cross "the world has been crucified to me, and I to the world" (6:14). According to Luke he exhorted (those same?) Galatians in the faith, "saying that through many tribulations we must enter the kingdom of God" (Acts 14:22). In Romans he wrote how God "sent His own Son in the likeness of sinful flesh and [as a sacrifice] for

32

sin" (8:3). In 1 Corinthians he recorded the traditional formula "that Christ died for our sins in accordance with the Scriptures," and "that He was buried, that He was raised on the third day in accordance with the Scriptures" (15:3–4), as he defended his preaching of salvation through the cross and resurrection of Christ.

Life through Jesus' death is the pattern for every Christian: "One has died for all; therefore all have died. And He died for all, that those who live might live no longer for themselves but for Him who for their sake died and was raised" (2 Cor. 5:14b–15, RSV).

Incorporation into Christ means a fusion of our selves with Him in His death: "Do you not know that all of us who have been baptized into Christ Jesus were baptized into His death?" (Rom. 6:3; cf. v. 5).

This general pattern holds true for Paul and for all Christians. But Paul also makes statements that go beyond this general principle. At times he speaks of his own actions and experiences as an apostle, a specially-set-aside minister, and there comes through a hint of his suffering and dying for others' sake. Not only is the *content* of his preaching the Gospel of life for all through the death of Christ, but also the *conduct* of his own ministry, as an apostolic imitator of the servanthood of Jesus, conforms to the pattern in which life is brought into being through suffering and death. The self-giving love that means life for others is stamped not only on Paul's words, but also on his ministry.

This comes to expression in a number of places. In a difficult passage, Paul says: "I bear in my body the marks (στίγματα) of Jesus" (Gal. 6:17). This may refer to the scars from beatings he received as an apostle, in which case the mystery of union with Christ is expressed in the experience of persecution and suffering. But it may also be a general reference to the way in which his ministry conformed to the pattern of Christ's, his Master's.

Paul understood that his being a prisoner was for the sake of the Gospel, so that his personal inconvenience and peril were for the sake of bringing the Word of life to others (e.g., to the praetorian guard, Phil. 1:12–14, 17; compare the earlier incident in Acts 16:19–34).

In a passage reminiscent of Moses' intercession for the people (Ex. 32:32), Paul offers to give up his own share of eternal life, were it possible, for the sake of his own kinsmen according to the flesh (Rom. 9:1–5).[6] This passage illustrates especially well how the stamp of the Servant's love is on the ministry of Paul, yet it does not detract from the uniqueness of Jesus as the Savior. It is *not* possible for unbelieving Jews to be saved through Paul's vicarious death for them.[7] It is not vicarious suffering in general that is redemptive. There is one name given under heaven by which humanity must be saved: Jesus. Only trust in *His* death saves. His is the once-for-all sacrifice for all sin, the only work needed to accomplish all that was necessary for reconciliation. But the *love* that led Him to it, and the *readiness* to suffer and die for others, indeed: involvement in the pattern of suffering and dying for others, is continued in the ministry of his apostolic imitators.

In a another passage, in which money-grabbing motives are being denied, Paul wrote to the Corinthians: "I will most gladly spend and be spent for your lives. If I love you the more am I to be loved the less?" (2 Cor. 12:15).[8]

This pattern of self-giving love, of death for life, stamped on Paul's ministry, is most remarkably expressed in two particular passages, 2 Corinthians 4:12 and Colossians 1:24. They deserve close attention.

2. 2 Corinthians 4:12

After considerable work to establish the Christian community in Corinth and after more than a year's absence from it, Paul heard reports of factionalism, immorality, wrong notions about the sacraments, the selfish use of spiritual gifts, the abuse of Christian freedom, and a misunderstanding of the doctrine of the resurrection in that congregation. These reports drew forth the response of 1 Corinthians and Paul's forceful presentation therein of the Gospel as the Word of the cross, which puts an end to the boasting of a theology of glory. The surprising truth is that, for all its brilliant persuasiveness, the sending of 1 Corinthians did not put an end to the troubles in the congregation at Corinth.

One way to ascertain the historical situation addressed by 2 Corinthians is to pose two questions: What, on the one hand, is different in the situation in Corinth as reflected in 2 Corinthians over against 1 Corinthians? On the other hand, how is the theme of 1 Corinthians, the theology of the cross, carried forward in 2 Corinthians?

In 2 Corinthians the focus has shifted to a great extent from the doctrinal and practical questions to the question of legitimate leadership. 2 Corinthians has been written after missions by Timothy (apparently) and Titus, as well as a painful visit and a tearful letter from Paul himself. A tremendous confrontation has taken place, and 2 Corinthians reports Paul's joy over Titus' report that Paul's point of view has prevailed. At the same time, the strong tone of chapters 10–13 suggests that Paul's opponents were still active, though now no longer in the majority; Paul presses for a completion of the "victory" over them.[9] It is clear in 2 Corinthians that since the time when 1 Corinthians was written, leaders had appeared in Corinth who were sharply opposed to Paul's apostleship and his preaching of the Gospel.

Who were these "superlative apostles"[10] who preached "another Jesus," a "different spirit," and a "different gospel" (2 Cor. 11:4–5)? It appears from 2 Corinthians 11:21–23 that they were Jewish Christians who claimed to be preeminent servants of Christ:

> But whatever any one dares to boast of—I am speaking as a fool—I also dare to boast of that. Are they Hebrews? So am I. Are they Israelites? So am I. Are they descendants of Abraham? So am I. Are they servants of Christ? I am a better one—I am talking like a madman . . . . (2 Cor. 11:21b–23a, RSV)

And from the phrase in 11:4, it appears that they were accepted as such: "You submit to it readily enough." They may well have had letters of recommendation (cf. 2 Cor. 3:1) from some leaders of the church in Jerusalem. 2 Corinthians 11:19–20 suggests that they were arrogant, aggressive, and authoritarian in their demeanor: "For you gladly bear with fools, being wise yourselves! For you bear it if a man makes slaves of you, or preys upon you, or takes advantage of you, or puts on airs, or strikes you in the face" (RSV).

They disparaged Paul, as the reference to their mocking his weakness shows (2 Cor. 10:10), and they may have even attacked him personally with verbal or physical abuse during his painful visit there (2 Cor. 2:5–11, although this interpretation is open to question).

Any further description of the opponents of Paul in Corinth generally runs in one of two directions,[11] and there is no general consensus as to which of the two is more likely. For the moment, however, it is not necessary to come down on either side of this debate, for the primary interest here is in a portion of Paul's defense of his apostleship in 2 Corinthians, and his main thrust comes across clearly regardless of whether he is directing it to the aberrations of proud Jewish Gnostics or to the claims to superiority of first-century Jewish-Christian Zionists. Faced with specific opponents who have challenged the legitimacy of his apostolic ministry and of his authority to correct the abuses in Corinth by his reemphasis of the Gospel as the Word of the cross, what does Paul say and do?

He makes several expected assertions. In 2 Corinthians 2:17 and 3:5–6 he claimed the divine origin of his apostleship and ministry. In conjunction with that, he introduced another idea (related to 1 Thess. 3:8): that the life of his converts in the new covenant is the proof (recommendation) of the validity of his apostleship. In 2 Corinthians 4:1–2 he emphasized his integrity in preaching God's Word, and in 2 Corinthians 11:7–9 he also referred to the self-sacrifice, including the financial self-sacrifice, which he had made for the sake of preaching the Gospel. According to Oostendorp,[12] this last passage said something that Paul's opponents could point to as evidence of Paul's incomplete understanding: Paul, as an Israelite, should have *demanded* financial support for himself from his Gentile converts; similarly, Paul's opponents would have found it strangely inconsistent for Paul to give up this right personally while at the same time gathering a collection from the Gentile churches for the saints in Jerusalem.

It is on this very point that the difference between Paul and his opponents rests, whether they be puffed-up Gnostics or proud "Christian Zionists." It is Paul's "weakness" that he points to as the proof of the legitimacy of his apostleship. In a remarkable procedure, he turns the accusation into the proof of his case. *They* have letters of recommendation, but how do *we* commend ourselves?

> As servants of God we commend ourselves in every way: through great endurance, in afflictions, hardships, calamities, beatings, imprisonments, tumults, labors, watching, hunger; by purity, knowledge, forbearance, kindness, the Holy Spirit, genuine love, truthful speech and the power of God; . . . (2 Cor. 6:4–7a, RSV)

They boast of their gifts and powers as servants of Christ; Paul (speaking as a madman) boasts of a long list of beatings and sufferings in

2 Corinthians 11:23–29, culminating in the point in 11:30 (reiterated in 12:5): "If I must boast, I will boast of the things that show my weakness" (2 Cor. 11:30, RSV). The reason for this Paul clearly states: "I will all the more gladly boast of my weaknesses, that the power of Christ may rest upon me. For the sake of Christ, then, I am content with weaknesses, insults, hardships, persecutions, and calamities; for when I am weak, then I am strong" (2 Cor. 12:9b–10, RSV).

This, then, is the way in which the theme of 1 Corinthians is carried forward in 2 Corinthians. When the focus of the issue shifts to the legitimacy of the apostle, then the theme of the theology of the cross becomes expressed in the theme of the sufferings and weaknesses of the apostle of the Crucified One. Precisely *these sufferings* testify to Paul's legitimacy in his office. Or, to say it another way, the legitimacy of the apostle of the Crucified One is corroborated by the extent to which his life as well as his preaching proclaims the Word of the cross.

This, then, is the historical and literary context of 2 Corinthians 4:7–12, a profound passage of special import to those set aside to serve in the holy ministry:

> But we have this treasure in earthen vessels, to show that the transcendent power belongs to God and not to us. We are afflicted in every way, but not crushed; perplexed, but not driven to despair; persecuted, but not forsaken; struck down, but not destroyed; always carrying in the body the death of Jesus, so that the life of Jesus may also be manifested in our bodies. For while we live we are always being given up to death for Jesus' sake, so that the life of Jesus may be manifested in our mortal flesh. So that the death is at work in us, and the life in you. (2 Cor. 4:7–12, RSV, except for the author's alteration of v. 12)

For the most part, this passage says the same things already enunciated in chapters 11 and 12, but perhaps a little more pointedly. Certainly the last verse, however, contains an unexpected twist: "so that the death is at work in us, and the life in you."[13] The suggestion of Adolf Schlatter leads to this translation of the definite articles, in the phrases ὁ θάνατος and ἡ ζωὴ, not as generic ("death" and "life") but as (anaphoric) references to the death and the life of Jesus.[14]

Members of the congregation in Corinth were enjoying spiritual gifts, but Paul continued to face sufferings. Did the difference signal that there was something wrong, something incomplete about Paul? No. In his *sufferings* it is apparent that the death of Christ is at work in him and in his ministry for them. In their *gifts* it is clear that the life of Christ is at work among them. But he and they are not thereby separated, for they are both of the same spirit of faith (2 Cor. 4:13) and will all be together in the resurrection of the dead (4:14). So all of Paul's suffering, as the apostle of the Crucified, "is for your sake" (4:15). Consequently, through his (persecuted) preaching of the cross "grace extends to more and more people" and enriches their life in Christ to "increase thanksgiving, to the glory of God" (4:15). While they are all clearly one in Christ, there is still this signal difference between the apostle, the one specially set aside and sent, and those to whom he is sent: "the death is at work in us, and the life in you."

3. Colossians 1:24

This same distinction appears in Colossians 1:24, a passage of considerable depth and difficulty. In response to the false teachings and false practices that had infected the Christian congregation at Colossae, Paul wrote a lofty testimony to Christ and a vigorous argument against alien rites.[15]

The first segment of the body of Colossians (1:13–29) deals with the Gospel of Jesus Christ and its work in the church through the ministry of the apostle.[16] Paul establishes first the preeminence of Christ, the Son of God, and then the all-sufficiency of His work of reconciliation. In Him the fullness of the Godhead dwelt bodily (1:19); no other spiritual entities need be dealt with as representatives of the divinity. In Him God was at work reconciling *all* things to Himself by the blood of His cross (1:20). The Colossians themselves have been included in the community of the reconciled through faith in the Gospel (1:21–23), preached to them by Epaphras (1:7) under the aegis of Paul's apostleship. This leads to a remarkable passage about Paul's apostleship, the Gospel ministry, and Paul's relationship to the Colossian Christians (whom, in fact, he has never met in person, 2:1):[17]

v. 24: who[18] [= I, Paul] am now rejoicing in
      my[19] sufferings for[20] you
   and fill up from my side[21] the measure
      remaining[22] of the afflictions
      of the Christ
   in my flesh for His body, that is, the church,

v. 25: whose[23] minister[24] *I* became
   in accord with the special role entrusted to
      me in God's plan of salvation[25]
   to fulfill with respect to you the Word of God:

v. 26: the mystery,[26] which was hidden
   from aeons and generations,
   now[27] has been manifested to His saints,

v. 27: to whom God willed to make known
   what is the wealth of the glory of this
      mystery among the Gentiles,
   which is:[28] Christ in you, the hope of glory,

v. 28: which[29] we proclaim, admonishing every man
   and teaching every man in all wisdom
   in order to present every man perfect[30]
      in Christ,

v. 29: toward which results I also toil,
   striving in accord with His working within me[31]
   which was worked in me in power.

Several observations may assist in the attempt to understand this passage. First, when verses 24–29 are read as prose, they appear to be a rather bad run-on sentence with an anacoluthon verse 26.[32] But Ernst Lohmeyer's analysis rings true[33] and helps to provide some clarity in the chain of thought. The arrangement of the translation above corresponds with his scheme of six subsections, of which five are begun with a relative pronoun.[34] These subsections deal with the following topics, which have a chiastic structure:

24 A   Paul's apostolic sufferings of the afflictions of the Christ
25 B   Are the direct result of the specific call to apostleship
        given Him by God.
26 C   The root of the call and the suffering is the revelation
        of the mystery in Christ.
27 C' The historical realization of the revelation of that mystery

          includes Christ in you, the Colossians.

28   B'   This historical realization entails a specific role and activity of Paul.

29   A'   Hence his present toil is in accord with and according to the pattern of the work of God, who is, indeed, the One working in him.

The chiastic structure calls attention to the reiteration of topics in the second section but, in each case, with a more specific application to the historical relationship of Paul and the Colossians. The correspondence of verse 29 to verse 24 suggests that the sufferings referred to in verse 24 do indeed have to do with God at work in Paul, as a called apostle, according to the pattern of His (God's) way of working.

Second, the "now" of verse 24 is quite stark if one does not read the "who" in front of it. Even with the relative pronoun connective, it is mildly emphatic. The question is, "now" in contradistinction to when? Is it future? Is it past? To what circumstances might it refer in the future or the past? One alternative is to paraphrase it: "Now, already during the time of suffering and not only first *after* the sufferings are over and I enter heaven, I am rejoicing." The opposite of "now" would be in the *future*. Another alternative is to see the opposite of "now" as in the past. Thus it could mean "now when I see the full extent of God's mercy, now when I ponder over His mighty work of reconciliation."[35] Or it may mean "now, after having been involved in the process of the afflictions, in contrast to the time when I first *became* a servant of the Gospel" (cf. v. 23). This last suggestion is probably preferable.[36]

Third, neither "sufferings" ($\pi\alpha\theta\acute{\eta}\mu\alpha\sigma\iota\nu$) nor "afflictions" ($\theta\lambda\acute{\iota}\psi\epsilon\omega\nu$) is Paul's term for what Jesus suffered in order to take away sin. That is expressed by "the cross," or "blood," or "death."[37] Almost all will agree, but nonetheless it needs to be reasserted very clearly that there is no question of this verse saying anything that would infringe upon the all-sufficient reconciling death of Jesus Christ.

Fourth, there is nevertheless a relationship between the apostle's suffering of the afflictions of the Christ, on the one hand, and "you," the "body of Christ," "the church," on the other hand. That relationship is described by one of those short troublesome words, the preposition $\acute{\upsilon}\pi\acute{\epsilon}\rho$: "for," "on behalf of," "in place of." Sufferings and afflictions are of benefit, and the benefit is *transferable*.[38] This is of prime import for understanding the passage.[39]

Fifth, the specific content of the sufferings and afflictions is not described. Paul makes no reference to any specific incident from his ministry. Precisely what experiences come upon an apostle is unimportant; what is important is that they are "for you." They are a divinely ordained necessity, which prepare for the eschatological day of Christ; hence, they provoke *joy*, for they hint at the coming glory of the Lord.[40]

Finally, the "afflictions of the Messiah" may be a technical phrase for the "messianic woes" (foreshadowed by the plagues in Egypt)[41] that will come, according to both late Jewish and Christian expectation, as part of the process of the coming of the Messiah.[42]

Broadly speaking, there are three lines of interpretation put forward to explain Colossians 1:24. Shorthand designations for them could be "mystical union," "messianic woes," and "apostolic ministry." Combinations, fusions, or overlaps are possible in some cases.

The "mystical union" line of interpretation takes seriously the indwelling of Jesus in His body, the church, on earth. The identification of Jesus and His church[43] becomes the rationale for saying that when a Christian suffers it is a continuation, of sorts, of the suffering of Jesus.[44]

There are at least two difficulties with this line of interpretation.[45] First, it is not here a matter of the *identification* of Paul and Jesus, but of their *distinction*.[46] Second, there is benefit for others in these sufferings.[47] This line of interpretation fails to note the strong emphasis on Paul's apostolic service in the context and does not take into consideration the full force of "on behalf of."

The "messianic woes" line of interpretation begins with the thought of an apocalyptic timetable that must be met. As in the Exodus, so also in the return of the Son of Man, there is a set period and pattern of tribulation and suffering: the "woes of the end-time," or the "messianic woes." Eduard Lohse suggests that Jewish notions of the end-time have influenced the early Christian expectation of the end and have been adapted here.[48] There is, supposedly, a set quantity of suffering to be gone through,[49] and so also a given amount yet remaining ($\dot{\upsilon}\sigma\tau\epsilon\rho\dot{\eta}\mu\alpha\tau\alpha$) to be filled up. Paul, who has been strengthened "for your encouragement" (2 Cor. 1:6)[50] and for whom his sufferings are a victorious service, is personally making his contribution to the filling up of the still-to-happen end-time afflictions. Thus he is helping to bring the dawn of the future glory that much closer, and this (according to Lohse) is how his suffering of the "afflictions of the Messiah" is of *benefit* to the Colossians.

This view has its own problems. It requires understanding the words "I fill up from my side" as "I make a contribution toward filling up." It is a contribution, moreover, that is in no way distinctive to the apostolic office. Every Christian who ever suffers anything would be, similarly, making his contribution toward this "filling up" for the benefit of others by bringing the day of consummation closer. In the context of Colossians 1:24, however, there is a strong emphasis on Paul's apostolic service.[51]

It is better, therefore, to take cognizance of that context and to follow the line of interpretation which ends with an emphasis on apostolic service and the ministry. This line of interpretation is followed, with various individual nuances, by Eduard Schweizer,[52] Ernst Lohmeyer,[53] and, with the claim to be rightly representing the position of Chrysostom, and Jacob Kremer.[54] Such an interpretation recognizes that Paul's suffering is immediately connected to his call into apostolic service (Acts 9:15–16!). It corroborates the above-given interpretation of 2 Corinthians 4:7–15, namely, that the weakness and sufferings of the messengers, the death at work in the apostle, lets the power of Christ and the glory of God truly shine through in the lives of the converts. It holds that the commission and the life of the apostle are one, so that also the proclamation and the suffering of the apostle are one.[55]

Although there can be no question of "adding to" or "completing" Christ's atoning work, this line of interpretation acknowledges that the apostle's suffering is of value for others. It is this suffering that first makes the message credible, letting the preaching become so real that faith comes to its fullness.[56] Indeed, through his apostolic ministry, in the period of the historical process *between* the resurrection of Christ and the return of the Son of Man, Paul continues the work that had its beginning in Christ. He continues, both before the world as well as to the congregation, what "has been completed eschatologically 'in heaven' and requires no further continuation."[57]

Typically provocative and to the point are the words of Ernst Käsemann, borrowed and framed by Erhardt Güttgemanns: "Paul is, with his σῶμα 'in his very person the manner of the appearing of the Incarnate Christ after his [Christ's] ascension into heaven.' "[58] In that he is the representative and imitator of his Lord, the apostle's sufferings take on the character of an epiphany: the revelation of the glory and strength of God in weakness.[59]

The key to understanding Colossians 1:24 lies in letting the ὑπέρ have its full force. Despite all the necessary measures to keep the all-atoning suffering of Christ distinct from the subsequent sufferings of Paul, Christ's apostle, one must find a way to let Paul's sufferings stand, differentiated at least in some degree from those of Christ *and* of benefit to the Colossians, indeed, of benefit to the whole body, the church.

Though a mystical union interpretation cannot stand, a sacramental union interpretation can. The suffering of Paul, the apostle, and the benefit to the church are at one in the sacramental union of Christ crucified at work in the institution of the ministry.[60] The same point, then, is made here as in 2 Corinthians 4:12: the death of Christ is at work in the ministry of his apostle.

4. A Concluding Proposal

Such an interpretation of these passages leads toward the vision of a great mystery about apostolic service and therefore also about the ministry. It has to do with the proclamation of the cross in the life and sufferings of the preacher as well as in his words.[61] It has to do with the relationship of the *events* of salvation to the *proclamation* of the events of salvation. It has to do with the working out now, in the historical situation of the interrelatedness of preacher-Gospel-and-hearers, those eschatological realities accomplished in Christ. It has to do with the ongoing process, between resurrection and Parousia, of God working that which He wrought in Christ. It has to do with God at work to save in Christ through the Gospel ministry of His apostles, a ministry of Jesus extended beyond the bounds of His earthly life.

Perhaps an analogy from the Old Testament will be helpful to set forth this vision. Sacrifice and blood-shedding are part of the typological prefigurement of the sacrifice of Christ and the re-demption won once for all by Him on Calvary. Nonetheless, those sacrifices are "for sin," and were carried out as such, by God's command, at a particular time and place. They had no meaning apart from the one eternally valid sacrifice for sin, but in connection with Christ they did carry the power of the atonement won by Him. Similarly, as regards the prophetic ministry, it is customary to speak of the sufferings of Jeremiah (as one example) as typologically prophetic (cf. Jer. 20:7–18). So also the sufferings of an apostle may be typological, not typologically prophetic, but typologically *imitative*, pointing not forward but backward to the Christ.[62]

This means that the ministry itself is sacramental in nature in the New Testament period, even as the this-worldly elements of the cultus and ministry in the Old Testament period were typological bearers of the power of God to save that would be revealed in the incarnate Christ. Pastors are human beings set aside, by divine institution, to be channels, proclaimers in word, deed, and in sufferings, of the Word of the Gospel of the crucified Christ. The sufferings of such set-aside men are the afflictions of the Christ; they participate in, typologically reveal, imitate, and so re-present in a given time and place that which was accomplished at Calvary on Good Friday for all times and places in Jesus Christ.

Therefore, apostles are not exactly the same as those who are not apostles; they have been singled out and given a specific role (οἰκονομία) in God's plan of salvation, and they have also been given the corresponding authority and responsibility of their office (ἐξουσία). Similarly, men in the ministry, set aside, also are not in every respect just like laymen. There can be no confusion: Peter is not Christ and Paul is not Jesus, and a pastor is not equal to the Lord. But those in the ministry are designated leaders,[63] targets for the world, lightning rods to the opposition, consecrated servants, mediators of the Gospel, and preachers of the crucified Christ in word, deed, and suffering. Theirs is a calling that imitates the pattern set by Jesus and so brings into being in historical situations between resurrection and Parousia the truth of the message of the one love that gave itself into death so that others might live.

This gives a far deeper meaning to the word "imitation." It gives new significance to the characterization of the holy ministry as "prophetic and apostolic." It is also a structure of theological understanding that allows the very best understanding of Colossians 1:24 and 2 Corinthians 4:12. As a living (and dying) sacramental imitation of the crucified Christ, the apostle Paul refers to what is being accomplished through his ministry as the "suffering of the afflictions of the Christ" "on their behalf." The death, Christ's death, is at work in *him*, so that the life, Christ's life, is at work in *them*.

C. Burnt Out—or Consumed?

Many speak these days about clergy burnout.[64] One wonders whether part of the problem is that too many people enter (or are allowed to enter) the ministry after having gotten "on fire for the Lord" in a shallow and non-understanding way. The passages presented above address this problem.

Our God *is* a consuming fire (Deut. 4:24; Heb. 12:29). But His is also a holy and sanctifying fire, which can burn without consuming that in which it appears (Ex. 3:2; Acts 2:3). Chaff and dross will be burnt away in judgment. That which is pure will abide. That which is burnt off needs to be burnt off. Perhaps some who are experiencing burnout are experiencing the burning out of their sinful ego's contribution to their understanding of the ministry.

The evangelist John says that this verse was true of Jesus: "Zeal for Thy house shall consume me" (Ps. 69:9; John 2:17). As is typical in the Gospel According to St. John, this verse has a meaning on several different levels. On the surface of the narrative, Jesus was showing Himself zealous for the house of God, that is, eager to see that the (second) temple not be abused. Therefore, He purged it of those keeping it from playing its proper role. On another level it was true that such zeal for God's house consumed Him, for by cleansing the temple He earned the enmity of the leaders of the Jewish religion and eventually was put to death. But, of course, Jesus' death was no accident. It was His own deliberate act fulfilling the plan of God. Zeal for God's house—the true building of the people of God, the church—was Jesus' "passion" for which He gave Himself and was consumed. Consumed, but not destroyed, for He was raised again on the third day.

If the new life of God's people is the passion to which today's pastor is zealously devoted, it will indeed *consume* him. It will do so in two ways. His sinful ego will be burnt up. (This is a good burnout.) But zeal for God's house can also be the passion of a pastor that "consumes" but does not destroy him; rather, it makes him new again in resurrection power. It is precisely the power of

God alone that accomplishes true ministry, sustaining him and making him equal to the task. He *will* be burnt up and burnt out, except to the extent that he is *truly* consumed with zeal for the Lord's house.

The Word of the cross works life. This truth can never be compromised. It must always be manifest in what a proclaimer of Jesus says and does and suffers. The life and the ministry of the new age go by new rules: "the ones who appear to rule the Gentiles lord it over them, and their 'great ones' exercise authority over them excessively, but among you it must not be so" (Mark 10:42–3). When confronted by those who put stock in the triumphalistic marks of power and success which characterize the old age, the imitator of Christ who would avoid burnout will point to his present "weaknesses" as testimony that the power of God is at work in the cross of the Crucified One whom he proclaims. Even when it is fellow Christians (or peers in the "ranks of the clergy") who, in their weakness, challenge him to play the game of authority and success, he "wins the cause" for himself and for them not by winning (as the world sees it) but by a manner of living that shows his trust in the power of the God who justifies the ungodly and who saves through the Word of the cross. For "the life" to work its effects in Christians, it is necessary that "the death" be at work also, specifically and especially in the the life and preaching of those who follow the apostles in the holy ministry.

The apostle Paul lays down this principle for the ministry: the preacher of the Gospel of God is uncompromising on the truth that the Gospel is the Word of the cross. He is uncompromising also in his acceptance of that truth as a pattern for his own life and ministry. A pastor validates and legitimizes his ministry not by pointing to all of his successes, but also by referring to his weaknesses and lack of power, his sufferings for the sake of the Gospel. When he is challenged, they testify to the legitimacy of what he has said and done in preaching the Word of the cross.

The pastor saves no lives unless he loses his own. For "the death is at work in us, and the life in you."

Chapter 4

A Divine Jealousy

A. Preservation

"Lord, keep us steadfast in Thy Word."[1] To be made alive is one thing. To be kept alive is another.

Everything that is true of the initial act of creation is also true of ongoing preservation, and everything that is true of the initial act of salvation is true also of preservation in the faith. Concern that those who have been brought to life (physical or spiritual) also be kept alive is part of God's work. Concern that those who have been brought into the faith are also kept in the faith is part of the work of God through the holy ministry. Martin Luther's familiar words make that abundantly clear: " . . . just as he calls, gathers, enlightens, and sanctifies the whole Christian church on earth and preserves it in union with Jesus Christ in the one true faith" (Small Catechism, Explanation to the Third Article of the Apostles' Creed). God does that watchful, preserving work through the ministry, men set aside to administer the means of grace, specifically, to preach the Gospel and administer the sacraments in accord with it.

1. Watchfulness Since the Beginning

The "living being" (*nephesh chayyah*) that the human being (*ha'adam*) became (Gen. 2:7) was precious to God. He had in him the breath of God, immediately given. God placed him in a garden and saw to it that his ongoing needs would be met.

But the man placed his own survival in jeopardy. Another master, one of whose names is "death," gained power over the man.

But the Lord God was jealous with regard to His breath, His Spirit whom He had caused to dwell in the man (James 4:5). That good divine jealousy motivated the plan of salvation: (1) victory over that enemy; (2) recovery (redemption) of humanity to live under the reign of the Creator; and (3) life of God and man in communion forever.

To arrive at that ultimate goal, God's jealousy had to remain ever watchful—and still must remain so until the end. The goal toward which that plan began to move with the Passover and the Exodus could never be attained without the pillar of fire and cloud in the desert, and without the quail and the manna and the water from the rock and the fiery serpent. It could not be attained without the continuing admonition and comfort of the priests and prophets.

Isaiah the prophet was performing this ministry of the jealous God when he laid before Ahaz signs and promises of God's powerful presence to sustain now and to preserve (or judge) forever when he assured him: "If you are not firm in trust, you shall not be made to stand firm."[2] And Habakkuk, in a verse programmatic for Paul and for the author of Hebrews,[3] likewise expressed the interplay between the posture of faith, being kept in the faith, and staying alive: "The one who is in a right relationship to God in a posture of trust shall, by his being kept in that faith, live."[4]

2. Jesus' Concern for Preservation

Jesus, having come and having called to Himself those given to Him by the Father, prayed for His own (John 17; esp. vv. 6, 9). He committed them to His Word and to the guidance of the "other Paraclete" (John 14:26; 15:26; 16:7–14). He spoke of the abiding union between God, Himself, and them, which results in that which was implicit from the beginning in His call to follow Him, "that where I am, there they may be also" (John 17:24).

3. Words of the Apostles Reflect This Same Concern

This same concern for protection in the right relationship to God so as to arrive at the goal of safety in heaven surfaces at many other places in the New Testament. St. Peter says: " ... be zealous to be found by Him without spot or blemish, and at peace" (2 Peter 3:14), and St. Jude enjoins: "Keep yourselves in the love of God: wait for the mercy of our Lord Jesus Christ unto eternal life" (Jude 21, cf. v.

24). In Revelation, St. John provides comfort for the persecuted and persevering saints (see chaps. 7, 12, esp. 12:14–16). St. Paul, as well, says: "The Lord is faithful; he will strengthen and guard you from the evil one" (2 Thess. 3:3).

B. Apostolic Ministry and Preservation of the Faithful in Paul

It is, indeed, an appropriate Biblical sentiment: to be concerned for others in their spiritual well-being, to encourage them to steadfastness, to pray for their preservation, and to cherish a desire to meet in heaven. But in this matter, again, Paul uses expressions that seem to carry the matter a few steps further.

Not just as the expression of an appropriate thought with regard to a fellow Christian, but as a statement made in consequence of his apostolic office, Paul says that *his* life now is sustained and *his* labor is vindicated in the end-time by the fact that his charges have been kept constant in the faith to the end. Once again, there is a special role, a special responsibility, and a special reward which belong to an *apostle*, and there is a special relationship that exists between an apostle and his charges.

Several of Paul's statements, understood in their historical and literary context, reveal yet another paradigm of ministry, rooted in the Biblical plan of God, revealed in Jesus and imitated by Paul.

1. 2 Corinthians 11:2

In another of his bold metaphors, Paul writes in 2 Corinthians 11:2: "I feel a divine jealousy[5] for you, for I betrothed you to Christ to present you as a pure bride to her husband."

The passion with which Paul opposed the false apostles in Corinth, the passion with which he struggled so that his converts might be kept in the faith, the passion which led to painful visit and tearful letter and foolish boasting is no human passion. It is rooted in Paul's sense of his own relationship to God and what God is doing through him. In 2 Corinthians 5:11 he had said: "Having known, therefore, *the fear of the Lord*, we persuade men . . . ."[6] It is no mere human venture that is under way. Having failed at this, one does not declare bankruptcy and start all over again. *This* is the ministry of the Word of life. Having failed at it one must cede ground to the enemy, death. Therefore, as Paul describes his reaction to the events transpiring in Corinth, he says that he was under such afflictions in Asia that he "despaired of life itself" and felt he "had received the sentence of death" (2 Cor. 1:8–9). Such is the desperation with which he strives to retrieve the faith and the souls of his Corinthian converts. Therefore his joy at Titus' report of their recovery (2 Cor. 7:6–13) is not only human emotion, but participates in that eschatological joy at the recovery of the lost, which has its counterpart among the angels in heaven.[7] *Now* he is confident of their life in the future *together* (2 Cor. 4:14; cf. 1:21), and he can point to them as *his* "letter of recommendation" (2 Cor. 3:2).

In all of this, he says, there has been at work in him a "divine jealousy," a zeal[8] of God. It is a concern for their well-being that is rooted in the desire to see the plan of salvation truly arrive at its ultimate goal: that they not be stolen away but be ensured safe to live with Him who loves them forever. As the apostle through whom the Corinthians were brought to faith, Paul feels a special responsibility for their preservation in the faith.

In the metaphor in 2 Corinthians 11:2–4, Paul is in the role of the father of a betrothed maiden. The betrothal took place when the Corinthians were converted. They are promised, now, to their Bridegroom, Christ, union with whom will be consummated at the last day when He returns. In the meantime they are to be kept pure and not, in disloyalty, be given into communion with any other (for example: the "different Jesus" being preached by the false apostles, v. 4). As their "father," it is Paul's responsibility, in his apostolic ministry, to ensure that they are kept in that pure and virgin state.[9] If he fails, the Word of life will have lost some ground to enemy death, and Paul will have less of a basis for appropriate pride[10] when he stands, as a steward, before Christ on the last day. Their preservation is his grave responsibility. The love of God constrains him to preach (2 Cor. 5:14), and the zeal of God constrains him to contend for the preservation of those who have been converted through his preaching.

2. Galatians 4:17

That same divine jealousy is behind the passionate outbursts in Galatians. Here, too, "disrupters" with "a different gospel" were attempting to snatch Paul's converts out of Paul's—and Christ's—hand, and Paul throws himself into the argument with all the ardor he can muster. The Galatians' survival in the true faith is what is at stake:

> I marvel that you are so quickly turning away from Him who called you in the grace of Christ [and] into a different gospel, which is not another gospel of the same sort as the true Gospel; [it is nothing other] except [that] there are some who are disturbing you and wishing to pervert the Gospel of the Christ. (Gal. 1:6–7)

As a corollary, the question of whether or not Paul's own toil is "in vain," "for naught," is also at stake: "I am afraid I have labored over you in vain" (Gal. 4:11).[11] In order that his own work stand the test of time, but even more importantly for their own sakes (cf. 2 Cor. 13:7), he must contend for the truth and for the preservation in the faith of the Galatian converts. When those whom he has betrothed to Christ are being courted[12] by others, Paul cannot sit idly by:

> *They* are zealous for you[13] not in a noble[14] way, but rather they wish to shut you out[15] in order that you might be zealous for them. Now, it is a good thing to have someone be zealous for you[16] in a noble way all the time, and not only while I am with you .... (Gal. 4:17–18)

Several points should be emphasized:

First, Paul's conflict is not with the Galatian Christians but with the (unnamed) "disturber(s)" (1:7; 5:12; 5:10). Here they surface again in the "they" of the verb forms and in the pronoun "for *them*." It is a logical assumption that these disturbers are of the same outlook as the "false brethren" referred to in Galatians 2:4.[17]

Second, Paul may well have been led in his choice of words by the historical background of the mission of the Judaizers. These Jewish Christians from Judea want to get the Galatian Gentile Christians circumcised in order that they themselves might avoid being persecuted (Gal. 6:12). They seek to look good and to gain a grounds for boasting in *their* (the Gentile Galatian Christians') flesh (6:13).

It is a most reasonable hypothesis[18] that these Judaizing Christians are motivated by pressures in Judea from Jewish forces of a "zealotic"[19] stripe. Such Zealotic activity was on the rise in the period after the death of Agrippa I and the arrival of procurators to govern

51

the new, larger province of Judea. In their "zeal for God" (a zeal also not characterized by understanding, cf. Rom. 10:2) these Jews were intent on purging the land of apostate Jews. Their zeal would be directed against Jewish Christians in Judea if they heard reports that Jews in that Christian "sect" kept fellowship with Gentile converts to Christianity who were not circumcised. Hence the irony when Paul says "they are zealous for you" "in order that you might be zealous for them;" the "zeal" of the "Zealots" is behind their zeal to have you circumcised, by which you Galatians will be doing *them* the favor of making them appear sufficiently "zealous" to the "Zealots."[20]

Third, obscured in the passive form in verse 18 (translated: "to have someone be zealous for you," but literally: "to be zealoused over") is the jealous love of God, who *is* zealous *nobly* and all the time. Such zeal of God, such divine jealousy, is at work in Paul's ministry when he is present with the Galatians and when he is not. The implication is that the Judaizers, who have hurried up to Galatia[21] in order to "make a big fuss" over them, will care not one whit about them after they shall have left. They have come only to get something done that will benefit themselves. Paul's concern stems from a genuine friendship that rests on a love for the truth.[22]

Finally, the truth is what is ultimately at stake, the truth that Paul tells and that the Judaizers (in their fear of persecution) obscure. This is the truth of the Gospel as the Word of the cross (cf. 5:11; 6:12).[23] It is not just that the Galatians are "Paul's" adherents, possessions of his whom he prefers not to lose.[24] The controlling power is not Paul, not even Paul in his (apparent to human eyes) apostolic dignity,[25] but the Gospel.[26] If Paul is constrained to preach the Gospel of Christ crucified (1 Cor. 9:16), he is equally constrained to defend the truth of the Gospel as the Word of the cross in all its implications and to *protect*, with a divine jealousy, those who through his ministry belong to the Gospel and to Christ crucified. This explains his noble zeal, the zeal of God in an apostle of God.

3. 1 Thessalonians 3:8

Nothing short of this same zeal lies behind 1 Thessalonians. Thessalonica is a strategic natural harbor located on the Via Egnatia, the highway from Rome to Byzantium. To this major crossroads Paul came, an apostle of Jesus Christ sent into Gentiles' territories. Paul was not the only one who came there with a message of "good news" from "god." Thessalonica was a regular stop for other traveling men with a message. Both teachers of popular religions (for the "simple") and also philosophers (gathering circles of the "wise") came and went through Thessalonica.[27] But, by the power of the Holy Spirit at work in the Word, the response of faith was kindled through the preaching of Paul (even if some of his statements may have been misunderstood, necessitating the further instruction contained in 1 and 2 Thessalonians). A community of Christians was called out of the world; an ἐκκλησία was brought into being in Thessalonica, born in the fires of persecution.

Acts 17 tells how the jealous(!)[28] Jews gathered together some of the rabble of the city and threatened trouble for Paul, who departed hastily for Berea, Athens, and then Corinth. Against his will, he was separated from his companions and from his new converts in Thessalonica.

Subsequently, Paul wrote from Corinth about himself and his ministry in relationship to the Thessalonian Christians. He was responding to the possible charge that he, after all, was really no different from any other traveling preacher of philosophy or spreader of ideas breeding social or political unrest: when the heat was on, he fled, leaving his unfortunate followers (like Jason) to suffer the consequences. Therefore, he makes it clear that he is not at all like those traveling charlatans (1 Thess. 2:3, 5–6). He calls on the Thessalonians to remember his scrupulous integrity both in financial matters and in interpersonal relationships (1 Thess. 2:9–12).

But Paul goes on, and once again says even more than one might expect. In an expression of emotion truly unusual in an ancient letter, he pours out his concern and his joy in 1 Thessalonians 2:17ff., culminating in a remarkable verse in 3:8:

> But since we were bereft of you, brethren, for a short time, in person not in heart, we endeavored the more eagerly and with great desire to see you face to face; because we wanted to come to you—I Paul, again and again—but Satan hindered us. For what is our hope or joy or crown of boasting before our Lord Jesus at His coming? Is it not you? Yes! You are our glory and joy. (1 Thess. 2:17–20)

For this reason, when I could bear it no longer, I sent that I might know your faith, for fear that somehow the tempter had tempted you and that our labor would be in vain.

But now that Timothy has come to us from you, and has brought us the good news of your faith and love and reported that you always remember us kindly and long to see us, as we long to see you—for this reason, brethren, in all our distress and affliction we have been comforted about you through your faith; for now we live, if you stand fast in the Lord. (1 Thess. 3:5–8, RSV)

All too easily passed by, these last words call for a closer look: "For now *we* live, if *you* stand fast in the Lord."[29] Greek grammar and lexicography can tell us several things about this sentence. "You stand"(στήκετε) is a present indicative form of a hypothetical verb (στήκω) derived, in Hellenistic Greek, from ἔστηκα, the perfect form of ἵστημι.[30] The first meaning of ἵστημι is transitive: "put, place, set."[31] As a present indicative, it is used (not classically) with a particle (ἐάν) to set up a condition that is a reference to a present reality:[32] "If it is true, as has been reported to me by Timothy (and I believe it!), that you are letting yourselves be made to stand firm in the Lord, then, consequently, we truly do live."

But how does one explain the "we live"? That is the real challenge. Some commentators see it in the arena of the human psyche: Paul means to say that he is happy at the news Timothy has brought him, that it has given him a new zest for his work. They point to Paul's disappointment in Athens and to his marking of time in Corinth until this news came, after which Paul's mission work in Corinth really "took off." He was, supposedly, psychologically down, and the news of the Thessalonians' faith "lifted his spirits" and gave him "a new sense of strength and joy, a life renewed in vigor . . . in moral and spiritual power."[33] It gave him a new lease on life.[34]

However, it is usually a mistake to limit the significance of Paul's words to the psychological realm. Behind his "moods" is a profound theological sensitivity for what *God* is doing. In connection with the life that God is establishing through Jesus Christ, namely, in a community of believers who are all members one of another in the body of Christ, the faith of the Thessalonian Christians is an essential part of Paul's own life with God in the body of Christ.

Paul's language about the church being the body of Christ is no linguistic device, a "mere" metaphor.[35] The life of one member is linked to and even dependent upon the life of the others—as, of course, the life of all the members is absolutely dependent upon the life of the head of the body, Jesus Christ. Thus it is justifiable to propose that in the "we live" in 1 Thessalonians 3:8 there lies an element of the eschatological life of Paul with God (which affects, in turn, his psychological energy for his work). As a Christian, and even more so as an apostle given the role of bringing about the obedience of faith within Gentile lands, Paul knows that the fullness and the quality of his life now and forever with God in the "communion of saints" is diminished if the Thessalonians fall away from the faith. But if they stand fast, his life is not diminished but enlarged and enriched and rewarded.[36]

Awareness of that eschatological enrichment is what, in fact, pumped new vigor into Paul for his work in Corinth. This dimension of the "we live" in 1 Thessalonians 3:8 is further corroborated by other verses in the same context. 1 Thessalonians 3:5 mentions a psychological state, specifically, fear. But the focus of the verse is on the last day and whether the tempter shall have succeeded in causing Paul's toil to have been "for naught." Similarly, verses 19 and 20 of chapter 2 place the whole matter of Paul and his converts into the perspective of the last day. These verses assert, by means of a rhetorical question and its answer,[37] that on the last day, at the Parousia of Jesus, the Thessalonian Christians will be for Paul a triumphal laurel wreath celebrating the accomplishment of what God set out to do through Paul.[38] Therefore, they are now already for Paul a source of hope and joy and of "glory."[39] Hence, Paul's "life" is connected to their being kept firm in the faith to the end. "Everything that a man might hold as important for himself Paul says that these Christians are and will be."[40]

4. A Steward—Not for Naught

An important reason for Paul's zeal and deep concern for the preservation of his converts to the end is his understanding that his apostolic work, as imitation of the ministry of Jesus, is to produce results that are to be visible on the last day. As an apostle,[41] Paul knows himself to be a steward, entrusted with a gracious and powerful gift (1 Cor. 4:1; Rom. 1:5). As every gift, this charism of apostleship brings with it a corresponding responsibility: a responsibility to work, to labor, to toil.[42]

Preaching is Paul's toil, and presenting saints brought through to the end is his goal.[43] Without this toil, that gracious gift bestowed upon him would accomplish nothing: it would be in vain and come to naught.[44] While every servant has equality in status (1 Cor. 3:8), the toils of each apostle are, like his *charismata* and his responsibilities, his own.[45] They shall be the basis for rewards (1 Cor. 3:8) and the proper kind of "pride," "joy," and "glory" on the last day.[46]

Even at that, his toil would come to naught if it did not bear fruit, namely: faith created through the Word in his preaching.[47] When his preaching has generated faith, then it has not been in vain (1 Thess. 2:1)—*unless* those believers should be tempted (1 Thess. 3:5), deceived (2 Cor. 11:3), or bewitched (Gal. 3:1) away from the true faith. Since it shall be his pride and joy to present them perfected, unblemished on the last day,[48] Paul is urgently concerned for his converts' preservation in the true faith, lest their absence from the communion of saints gathered on the last day demonstrate that his toil[49] had been for naught.[50]

Thus having only done his toil of preaching is not enough for Paul.[51] He has no choice but to preach (1 Cor. 9:16), yet he has nothing to point to with proper pride of accomplishment if he just preaches. It provides him no reward, no basis for a proper boasting, joy, or glory. However, when he has freely given up what was due him (for example, his right to be supported by those to whom he preaches) he can be "proud" (1 Cor. 9:15; 2 Cor. 11:10). The present fruits of his labors, his congregations' faith and love and generosity, are subjects of which Paul boasts to other men (2 Cor. 7:4, 14; 2 Thess. 1:4). Of himself, as we have seen, he now boasts only of his weaknesses (2 Cor. 11:16–30). But on the last day, Paul's behavior in the ministry now will be a reason for pride and joy to his churches and, correspondingly, his converts will be a basis of pride for him (2 Cor. 1:14).[52]

Thus the interpretation of 1 Thessalonians 2:20 given above is corroborated by a whole pattern of the interrelationship of the believers' preservation in the faith and perseverance to eternal life and Paul's own life and joy and glory. This is brought out in all its forthright beauty in Philippians 2:16: "[... that you may be] ... holding fast the word of life, so that in the day of Christ I may be proud that I did not run in vain or labor in vain." (RSV)

On these words of Paul concerning those beloved Philippians, his "joy and crown" (Phil. 4:1), Ernst Lohmeyer aptly comments: [53]

> It is *not* true that the "perfection" of the ethical-religious life (as it has been established in the church by God and makes itself evident in the church's action) is the "pride" of the apostle *only* in an empirical historical sense; rather, the church's "perfection" is also the apostle's "pride" in the sense of an eschatological necessity. For "pride" is a signal of the task completed and of the divine gift preserved intact "on the day of Christ." Every believer has this "pride" to bear in and of himself; but it is inherent in the meaning and goal of Paul's apostleship that for him the confession of his own life is not enough, but rather the confession of the congregations founded by him is also necessary. Thus, under this consistent eschatological point of view, apostle and congregation grow together into a unity that is indissoluble in life and in death. Just as the congregation can never be nor act without its apostle, so also the apostle can neither be nor act without his congregation. The apostle's life spends itself in the congregation's existence; and the congregation, present on the day of Christ, owes its existence precisely to its apostle. Therefore the whole work and life of the congregation is "to his glory." This grand conception throws an illuminating beam on Paul's whole life's work (as becomes clear in vs. 16c). All the urgency and trouble of his life, the passionate struggles for the survival of his congregations, have their foundation in the question which the day of Christ poses to him: whether "I ran in vain or toiled in vain." It is the question of the religious meaning of his life, and it is equivalent to the question of the religious meaning of his work. This, then, brings up the need, for one last time, to imitate the example of Christ. Just as, in the end-time, Christ, as Lord, does what he is and is what he does—the very name "Lord" says precisely this—so also with the apostle being and work belong together. In the former case (of Christ), it has been accomplished as a timeless paradigmatic fact; in the latter case (of Paul), it still is straining toward its realization "on the day of Christ."

This venerable commentator has here woven together all the themes of this chapter: in imitation of Christ the apostle Paul identifies his being and his work, his mission and his fate. His "life" is unthinkable apart from the fruit of his labors. His service as a missionary and as a curator of souls culminates in this priestly offering, to present his charges as a spotless offering on the last day (cf. Rom. 15:16). To accomplish this means to celebrate the victory of life; to fail means to cede territory to death, and to know its sentence.

Not to accomplish this will be to have failed in his stewardship, in his apostleship, in his life's work. Not to accomplish this will be to have to live with the disappointment of souls lost, the communion of saints diminished by absent ones. Not to accomplish this will be to have lost something of the fullness of the life, the peace, the wholeness that ought to have been.

This sense of eternal oneness in Christ with his converts moved Paul to be determined not to lose those entrusted to him. This zealous determination is the mirror-image of the strong love of God, which wills not to cede the breath of life He has put into man to the rule of the enemy, and which will not let any of the recovered elect in Christ be snatched out of His hand. Such a love, such a divine jealousy, drove Paul to write, visit, admonish, and encourage his churches and to defend them from all that could prove hurtful to their faith and their eternal salvation. His ministry became the means of the operation of the powerful grace of God to keep all believers "united with Jesus Christ in the one true faith."

C. The Life You Save May Be Your Own

"No man is an island, entire of itself; each is a piece of the continent, a part of the main." John Donne's poetic insight about humanity is true all over again of those who are made alive anew in Christ. Those who have been set aside into the holy ministry to be vehicles for the nurture and preservation of the life of others will do well to remember it. Each parishioner is a member of the body of Christ, a saint with whom the pastor is one in Christ. The spiritual strength or weakness of any one individual affects the life of the whole body. No part of the body, requiring care, can be neglected without detriment to the entire organism. The leader must know that and know of his unity with every member in that member's needs and weaknesses: "Who is weak, and I am not weak? Who is made to fall, and I am not indignant?" (2 Cor. 11:29).

Parishioners are a trust, a treasure, a stewardship. Too often pastors, for various reasons (some of which may be caused by the laity themselves) are afraid of their parishioners, as though the congregation, or the elders or some such body, were their "bosses." Too often pastors, again for various reasons, are tired of their parishioners, as though the parishioners were all pesky children. Too often pastors are frustrated with their congregation, usually because of a lack of vision of what the church is, as though it were a computer which they cannot quite get programmed to function the way they want it to.[54] In reality parishioners are a trust, a stewardship, an opportunity for service: they are the task and therefore a part of the life and being of the pastor himself.

Each member of a congregation—no, let us go beyond the membership rolls, every person who comes into contact with a pastor—deserves to receive from him the ministry of the Word of God. Each such person is an encounter which provides for that pastor an opportunity for gathering more fruit to be a sacrificial offering on the last day. Each such person is to be protected, defended, encouraged, strengthened, nurtured, and kept in the faith. He needs to serve them, each one of them, one by one, as though he were one with them forever. He is.

Of course, this nurturing, protecting, and keeping is not done by the pastor's own power, but by God's power at work in the Gospel through him. But it does not happen apart from the pastor's own commitment, his own mirroring of the divine love, the divine jealousy.

Reclaiming the pattern of the divine jealousy that Paul provides can strengthen this vision of the ministry. He shows that, for those who have been entrusted with the responsibility of the spiritual care of others, there has been set between them and their charges a bond that unifies them and affects the fullness and the richness of their own life with God in the communion of saints. A minister's hope of glory (καύχησις, that *appropriate* sense of worth), joy, and life in the age to come depends also on the presence there of those whose care was his responsibility. Their loss means to know the sentence of death; their standing fast means his life.

Each pastor reflects the love of God in a divine jealousy over his parishioners, and he should say of his congregation: "Now I live, if you stand fast in the Lord." Each pastor should preach and teach and care for them believing absolutely that this is true. To twist a well-known phrase into a barely acceptable theological application, "the life you save may be your own." Such parishioners, kept safe by the Holy Spirit through his ministry, may be *now* a source of support and a confirmation of his calling (his letter of recommendation) as well as something to offer to the King to show the fruits of his toil on the last day.

There is a noble way to be zealous, jealous, and solicitous over someone (Gal. 4:18): with the divine jealousy that spares no effort to ensure that its treasure is not lost. Spare no efforts, pastors, as curators of souls. Be zealous that on the last day you may step forward, as an undershepherd reporting to the Chief Shepherd and Guardian of Souls and say: "By Your power and authority, Sir, Your servant delivers to You safely this contingent of Your church: All present and accounted for!"

Chapter 5

Blessed Peacemakers

A. War and Peace

God gave to man his rightful place in God's garden (Gen. 2:15, 19–20). Man's relationship to everything other than God was determined from the beginning by his relationship to God (Gen. 2:16–17). When the vertical relationship went askew, the horizontal relationships could not remain stable. The disobedience of sin broke the relationship of trust and dependence between human beings and God and simultaneously brought the accursed consequences of fear, competition, and domination into the relationships between humans and everything else (Gen. 3:16–19). Sinners are competitors; they are not their "brother's keeper" (Gen. 4:3–9). Man's removal of himself from a right relationship to God caused the entire creation to be subjected to futility.[1]

1. The Promise

Correspondingly, the promise of peace is a word that holds out hope for a restoration, within the context of a restored relationship to God, of peace in all other relationships as well. *Shalom*, unthinkable apart from peace with God,[2] is a word of completeness and wholeness.

Hence the Prince of Peace (Is. 9:6) is promised as Prince not only of a peace between God and man, but also as Prince of a peace between man and man and for man and the rest of creation. In His day there shall be a perfect new covenant of peace between God and His people, unbroken, characterized by full communion and knowledge, established by ("for," *ki*, v. 34) the forgiveness (forgetting) of sins.[3] In His day the world of nature, rendered sterile and savage under God's judgment (Is. 34: esp. vv. 3, 7, 9–15), shall be restored to its joyous harmony (Is. 35:1–2, 9; Is. 11:6–7) and shall be no threat to humanity (Is. 11:8–9). In that day nations shall seek the root of Jesse, the ensign to the peoples, and old hatreds shall be overcome so that God's plan to gather His people whole and complete, one in Christ, shall be accomplished (Is. 11:10–13).

2. The Prince

The ministry of the forerunner, John the Baptist, anticipated the light from on high, "to guide our feet into the way of peace" (Luke 1:79). So it was that He, the Prince of Peace, Light to the Gentiles and the Glory of Israel (Luke 2:32), was worshiped by Judean shepherds (Luke 2:8–20) and Magi of the East (Matt. 2:1–12). Jesus carried His ministry into Gentile territories (e.g., Mark 7:24, 31) and did not withhold His saving power from non-Jews (e.g., Luke 7:1–10; 8:26–39; 17:11–19), thus revealing that He, when lifted up on the cross, would indeed draw all people to Himself (John 12:32, which answers vv. 20–21). In drawing them to Himself, He also draws them to each other (cf. John 17:20–23).

He described what it really means to "be your brother's keeper" in the illustration known as the "good Samaritan" (Luke 10:25–37). He taught His disciples to pray: "And forgive us our debts, as we also have forgiven our debtors" (Matt. 6:12, RSV). This forgiveness is *the way of life* for those who live in the kingdom into which one enters only by receiving the forgiveness of his *own* sins. Jesus makes precisely this point in the parable of the "unmerciful servant" (Matt. 18:23–35). Jesus taught very clearly concerning "horizontal" reconciliation in his kingdom:

> If, then, you should be offering your gift at the altar and there should remember that your brother has something against you, leave your gift there before the altar, and go, first be reconciled to your brother and then come and offer your gift. (Matt. 5:23–24)

"Blessed," He said, "are the peacemakers" (Matt. 5:9).

3. Apostolic Peacemakers

The apostles continued this admonition of Jesus, reminding their hearers of the restored fellowship between men that results from the restoration of peace with God. St. Peter, who had reminded the Jews that the promise was to them and to their children "and to all that are far off, every one whom the Lord our God calls to him" (Acts 2:39), exhorted the "exiles of the dispersion" (1 Peter 1:1) to "put away all malice" (2:1) and to "love one another earnestly from the heart" (1:22; cf. 2:17; 3:8; 4:8–9). In a quotation of Psalm 34 (vv. 12–16), he urged his readers to seek peace (1 Peter 3:11), and in his second epistle he wrote: "Be zealous to be found by Him without spot or blemish, and at peace" (2 Peter 3:14). For "the wisdom from above is . . . peaceable," and "the harvest of righteousness is sown in peace by those who make peace" (James 3:17–18). St. John also admonishes that "if He so loved us, we also ought to love one another" (1 John 4:11), and the author of Hebrews urges us to "pursue peace with all" (Heb. 12:4).

B. The Gospel of Reconciliation in Paul[4]

Throughout his epistles St. Paul also proclaimed the establishment of peace with God in Jesus Christ and the concomitant results of peace between men and the hope for harmony in the fullness of the new creation.

1. The Gift of Peace

Peace with God is the possession of those who have been justified through faith in the Lord Jesus Christ,[5] in whom God was at work, making peace through the blood of His cross (Col. 1:20), and thus reconciling the world to Himself (2 Cor. 5:19; cf. Rom. 5:10–11). This peacemaking power of the Gospel has consequences, according to Paul, in the horizontal relationship of men and the world. It establishes the hope of wholeness for all creation, and it lays before Christians the call to unity.

2. The Hope of Wholeness

Paul touches upon the cosmic aspect of salvation in Romans 8:18–25.[6] In connection with the restoration of human beings to a right relationship to God, as His sons, there is also hope for the rest of the creation to be released from its bondage to decay. For the nonhuman creation, too, has been subjected to futility as the result of God's judgment upon man's sin, and its release ("redemption") from such futility will come about through the restoration of human beings to their rightful place and posture as sons of God. When God restores peace between Himself and humanity, He also reconciles to Himself the whole universe (τὰ πάντα, Col. 1:20). All creation is made whole again under God and his "son" and agent, man.

This wholeness is not yet a reality, as the disruptive effects of man's sin are all too evident in the unmanageable environmental problems of this "old world."[7] But when what only faith can now see shall become evident, namely, "the unveiling of the sons of God" (Rom. 8:19), the free and harmonious new heaven and new earth will also appear (Rev. 21:1). The key word *now* is "hope" (Rom. 8:24).

3. The Call to Unity

The implementation of peace between individuals is also part of the practical task now set before believers in Christ who have received the gift of peace with God. Paul's typical exhortation included the urging that the Christians be "of one mind," "the mind of Christ" (Phil. 2:2, 5). He encourages the Romans to live in "harmony" with one another in Christ (Rom. 12:16; 15:5), to "welcome" one another (Rom. 15:7),[8] to strive for the things that pertain to peace (Rom. 14:19), and to be at peace with all people, "in so far as it depends on you" (Rom. 12:18). In Ephesians Paul proclaimed the boldest and clearest lesson of the horizontal consequences of the peace established in Christ: unity in Christ, even of Jew and Gentile.

> For He is our peace, who has made us both one, and has broken down the dividing wall of hostility, by abolishing in His flesh the law of commandments and ordinances, that He might create in Himself one new man in place of the two, so making peace, and might reconcile us both to God in one body through the cross, thereby bringing the hostility to an end. (Eph. 2:14–16, RSV)

It was part of Paul's special role to elucidate this particular horizontal consequence of the Gospel (Eph. 3:1–6).

4. "Charge It to My Account"[9]

Not only did Paul proclaim and exhort to peace, but his personal posture in the "ministry of reconciliation" (2 Cor. 5:18) supplies a paradigm of ministry as a peacemaker. Philippians preserves his urgent appeal to Euodia and Syntyche that they should be at one in the Lord (Phil. 4:2). Romans records his offer, were it possible, to be anathema himself in order to effect the restoration of his kinsmen by race (Rom. 9:3). But it is the precious (but neglected) little Epistle to Philemon that gives the most impressive record of Pastor Paul in action in the ministry of reconciliation. Here Paul not only preaches peace, not only exhorts to peace, but gives of himself to *make* peace.[10]

Onesimus, the runaway slave, has found his way to Paul, who is in prison. People hold various views as to whether the scene of this meeting was Ephesus, Caesarea, or Rome.[11] Wherever it may have been, it is unlikely that Onesimus "just happened to wind up" where Paul was, as if by chance. It is more probable that Onesimus purposely went straight to Paul, who, he realized, was the highest earthly authority for the religion of his master.

E. R. Goodenough has documented a type of "asylum" practice regarding runaway slaves about this time in Egypt,[12] and this could be the legal background for what Onesimus thought to do in fleeing to Paul. A runaway slave, Goodenough says, could take refuge in a local temple, or even at the altar of the household gods of a neighboring householder. Then the temple authorities, or the neighboring householder, had the responsibility of reconciling the runaway slave to his master. This often involved the settling of a grievance or a misunderstanding (not that the slave, however, had any "bargaining" rights). If that attempt to effect reconciliation failed, this "mediator" had the responsibility of selling the slave on the market and turning the price over to the former owner. Slaves tended to accept the terms of the offered reconciliation, Goodenough says, because to be auctioned off as a runaway usually resulted in a far harsher servitude than that of being a householder's slave.

If this custom also prevailed in Asia Minor in Paul's day, one could well understand why Onesimus, having run away, would seek out Paul in the hope that the apostle, whom Philemon accepted as religious authority, would be able to effect a reconciliation.

With this possible background, we find that when this epistle is written Paul is in prison and Onesimus is with him, having now himself been converted to the Christian faith. The situation presented Paul with an opportunity for apostolic ministry, the ministry of reconciliation. Typically, he seized the opportunity.

He appealed to Philemon on the basis of the love of God[13] to do what is right and receive the runaway back again. Within the epistle there are a few (not so?) subtle hints and reminders of the relationship of Paul and Philemon (who had never met in person) with regard to Philemon's life in the Gospel in the new age: " . . . though I am bold enough to command you to do what is required . . . —to say nothing of your owing me even your very own self" (vv. 8, 19)[14]

But the main thrust of the appeal is on the basis of the Gospel, the love of God and the mercy of God shown to all three (Paul, Philemon, and now Onesimus, too) and the brotherhood between them all that the Gospel has created. This is all very proper, very much what one would expect Paul to do.

In fact, however, the nature of his apostolic ministry as imitation leads him to go a step farther in his action to effect this reconciliation. "So if you consider me as one having fellowship [with yourself] receive him into fellowship [with yourself] as [you would] me" (Philemon 17). Here there is laid down almost a substitutionary principle, which also comes to the surface in verse 12: "I am sending him back to you, sending my very self."[15] An extension of this same principle leads to the kind of thing that Paul says in verse 18, "If he has wronged you at all, or owes you anything, charge that to my account."

"I am sending my very self." "Charge it to my account." These things could have been said by Jesus Christ for every one of us.[16] The reconciling work of Christ is the basis and also the *model* for Paul's apostolic ministry. In an imitation of Christ, Paul offers himself in order to effect reconciliation, to make peace, between Onesimus and Philemon. Because of the nature of the brotherhood established by the Gospel and because of the imitative quality of the apostolic ministry, Paul cannot possibly make a merely formal request or appeal. In the ministry of reconciliation he puts his own self and his own goods "on the line" in order to accomplish the reconciliation of two Christians. Furthermore, he also instructs Philemon to see his slave (who is still his slave) in a new light, as a Christian *brother* (Philemon 16), as one in a new relationship to him, a relationship that transcends (even if it does not now abolish) and transforms the relationship of master and slave.[17]

The point for the office of the apostolic ministry is clear: the pattern that Paul follows is the pattern of Jesus himself. He is ready to say "charge it to my account" in order to bring about reconciliation. He offers himself as "surety."[18] It is, in miniature, a recapitulation of *the* reconciliation.

C. Blessed Peacemakers

Those appointed to serve in the footsteps of the apostles, in the holy ministry, need to observe and to imitate this pattern for ministry. Reconciliation, wholeness, unity, and harmony among the people of God are part of the expected results of the work of God in Christ through his ministers. The ministers are to be peacemakers, and the love of God, which alone can truly make peace, is to fill their ministry even as Jesus' ministry manifested it, and Paul, through apostolic imitation, continued it.

"Talk," the saying goes, "is cheap." This is true of the word of man. But the Word of God also *does* what it says. Proclaimers of peace, by the power of God's love, also act to establish peace. Ministers of reconciliation do not just talk about reconciliation; they bring it to pass. They bring it into being through their ministry through their preaching of the Gospel and administration of the sacraments. They bring it about also in the sense of making it practically effective in individual instances, through their own loving, mediatorial efforts as curators of souls.

"Put your money where your mouth is," goes another old saying. The pastor does not just urge the people of God to be of one mind as brothers and sisters in Christ in the life of the new age; he makes present the self-giving love that establishes the basis for that kind of unity and peace. He "puts his heart into it" and "gets involved"— personally involved, viscerally involved (cf. Philemon 12). He is ready to put himself in the gap (Rom. 9:3) and his goods on the line (Philemon 18). The calling includes the call to self-sacrifice.[19]

The minister of the Gospel and servant of Jesus Christ is not a professional in the tradition of "have gun, will travel": a detached, efficient pro who is so good at what he does that people pay him to do it. There is no room here for slick performers, detached counselors, hired hands. This is not the calling for nine-to-five paper-pushers, schedule-makers, and people-manipulators. No. The minister of the Gospel and servant of Jesus Christ is a professional in the tradition of the old town doctor: the person who does what he does because he is who he is and happens to get paid for it (more or less), even though he would do all the same things even if he did not get paid.[20]

Sometimes pastors have the opportunity to be living mediators between estranged Christians. They need to recognize it as in their calling and responsibility to seize such opportunities. The spending of one's own time and emotional energy will be involved (2 Cor. 12:15), and it may cost some personal loss. This is one more way in which "the death" is at work in the ministry in order that "the life" of peace restored may be at work in the church (2 Cor. 4:12). Thus Christian ministers, in the ministry of reconciliation, imitate Paul, the imitator of Christ, when they make peace by saying: "Charge it to my account."

Chapter 6

To Be Like God

Imitation, it is said, is the most sincere form of flattery. Holy Scripture attests the truth of this old saw.

A. Scripture's Testimony on "Being Like God"

God created the human being as a creature in His own "image" and "likeness" (Gen. 1:26). Man was made to be a mirror-reflection of God's holiness and glory. Sin consisted in man's desire to "be like God" apart from the relationship of creaturely trust in and obedience to the good Creator (cf. Gen. 3:5).

All that follows in Scripture is the story of what God has undertaken to do in order to recall man from his blasphemous attempt to usurp God's place and to restore him to that relationship in which man is again "like God" as God's creaturely image. Man was not made to be the originator of holiness and glory; he was made to be an imitator (μιμητής)[1] of God.

Therefore, God's judgment rolled down upon all those who would marshal human forces to storm God's heights, tower-builders from Babel and from all other times and places down to the present day. But the promise came as well: the promise of the Man in whom all humanity would see God, receive God's glory, and be God's sons and friends and imitators. The promise of such restoration in Jesus Christ went out for all who stood in the right posture in the creature-Creator relationship, the posture not of an aggressive tower-builder but rather of a trusting recipient of grace.

1. The Law and the Prophets

Nothing other than this is expressed in the famous verse: "You shall be holy, for I the Lord your God am holy" (Lev. 19:2, RSV). Therein lies a word of Law against all that keeps itself separate from God's holiness. But therein lies also a promise: "You *shall be* holy!"

Nothing other than this is being promised when God, through the prophet Isaiah, describes His servant, Israel, as the One "in whom I will be glorified" (Is. 49:3). In an elect Servant, holy and blameless, God will again have His mirror-image, His imitator, reflecting His glory.

2. The Son, the Glory of the Father

When the appointed time had arrived, the sinless, holy Servant, the true Son of God, came into the world. Jesus was God's Son in essence (Luke 1:30–35). He was the faithful Servant of the Lord, the true Israel, Israel reduced to one, who accomplished everything that the people Israel had been called to do but had failed to do.[2] In obedience He maintained a perfect unity with the will of His Father (Matt. 4:1–11; John 5:19, 30). The glory of God shone forth from Him (Luke 9:29–32; John 1:14; 12:27–8; cf. John 18:6) and was reflected by Him in obedient sonship (John 17:1–5). His divine sonship and holiness were attested to by spirits (Mark 1:24) and (Spirit-inspired) men (Matt. 16:16; John 6:69). He Himself said: "He who has seen Me has seen the Father (John 14:9).

He called and taught disciples. "Follow me!" he said, in effect: "Become a disciple, a learner."[3] "Learn from Me, for I am gentle and lowly in heart" (Matt. 11:29, RSV). "I have given you an example," He said (John 13:15), and: "You are the light of the world (Matt. 5:14), . . . let your light so shine before men that they may see your good works and give glory to your Father who is in heaven" (Matt. 5:16, RSV). Be pure in heart; see God (Matt. 5:8). Bring glory to His name by your behavior (in Christ) that shows the blessedness of a life that trusts in His grace and obeys His will.

3. Apostolic Testimony to the Chain of Likeness

All of his apostles taught the same thing. They identified Jesus as the Son of God (1 John 1:3; Heb. 1:3; 5:5; 2 Peter 1:17). They told those being saved in Christ that they were "saints," "holy ones," and even "partakers of the divine nature,"[4] in order to bring glory to Him who created and saved them (1 Peter 2:12; 2 Peter 3:18). Therefore they should lead lives worthy of their calling, holy, as He who called them is holy (1 Peter 1:15; 2 Peter 3:11). For they will be, as His children, *like* Him (1 John 3:1–3). Now they should "imitate not what is evil but what is good" (3 John 11), and, when appropriate, they can even be exhorted to imitate their leaders (Heb. 6:12; 13:9).

B. The Imitation of Christ in Paul

The idea of imitation, and of enjoining behavior by calling for imitation, is an ancient one.[5] But though the idea is part of the mental furniture of the Hellenistic world, Paul—a Roman citizen, Greek-writing Jew, and Christian apostle—stands squarely in the tradition of the Old Testament, Jesus Christ, and the Christian apostles on this subject.

1. Reiteration of Apostolic Testimony

Paul repeated the same kind of testimonies and exhortations as the other apostles. He too spoke of Jesus as the Son and image of God, from whose face shines God's glory (Rom. 1:3; Col. 1:15; 2 Cor. 4:6). He too considers the Christians as saints (1 Cor. 3:16–17), sons in Christ, whose destiny is to be conformed to the image of Christ (Rom. 8:29) and who are to attain to the glory of the sons of God (Rom. 8:15–25). Paul, as the others, admonishes those who are in Christ to show forth holiness as the fruit of the Spirit's power at work in their lives, renewing and transforming them from the inside out (Rom. 12:1–3).[6] He tells them to lead lives worthy of their calling (Eph. 4:1), to be holy and blameless, shining as a light in the midst of a perverse and crooked generation (Phil. 2:14–17). He tells them to put on, in Christ, the new nature created "in the likeness of God" (Eph. 4:22–24), and so to become imitators and reflectors of God, as beloved children.[7] He describes, too, how they are transformed from glory to glory when they look upon and reflect (κατοπτριζόμενοι) the glory and the image of the Lord (2 Cor. 3:18).

2. The Apostle as Paradigm

St. Paul did more than reiterate attestations and exhortations. In his own person he described and in his own deeds he put into action an example of the consequences of his proclamation. "Be conformed to the image of Christ" means more than "doing" individual "good works," and also more than waiting for felicitous accidents to kick along a meandering process of spiritual evolution. For Paul "be conformed" and "be transformed" mean war; the war of the Spirit against the flesh, the war of sanctification that rages within every simultaneously-saint-and-sinner-Christian who is still in this world. It calls for a power from within, specifically, for self-discipline and obedience in the new man. Even more, it calls for power from without: the Holy Spirit *transforming* the person and *conforming* his behavior to a certain standard.

The standard is described in the Word of God. It is incarnate in Jesus. It is also exemplified in the apostle. Paul boldly puts himself into the picture again. Part of his ministry was to be able to set himself up as a paradigm and to say such things as: "Brethren, become (joining together with others) imitators of me,[8] and keep your eyes on those who are conducting themselves thus, just as you have us as an example" (Phil. 3:17).

It is instructive to examine more closely the circumstances and context of several passages in Paul's letters where he does this.

A. 1 THESSALONIANS 1:6 (CF. 2:14)

" . . . and you[9] were made to be[10] imitators of us and of the Lord, having received[11] the Word amid[12] great tribulation with (the) joy of[13] the Holy Spirit." Chapter 4 has already described the broader historical context of 1 Thessalonians. This verse appears in the formal thanksgiving, in which Paul is recalling those events that have established his relationship with the Thessalonian Christians, namely, his preaching and their faith.

Here, as in 1 Thessalonians 2:14,[14] Paul makes an indicative declaratory statement in the aorist: "you were made to be";[15] thus, the reference is to the time and circumstances of their conversion. Specifically, the Thessalonian Christians were "made to be" "imitators" through the confluence of three circumstances: first, they welcomed the Word (i.e., they came to faith); second, this occurred in the midst of tribulation;[16] and third, they did so with the joy that is "inspired by"[17] the Holy Spirit.

Their being "imitators" is therefore not entirely a matter of their own action. It is not simply that "the Thessalonian Christians" are the subject of an active verb, "imitate." It is a matter of the pattern of a whole set of circumstances in which the Thessalonians are both active and passive: they "become" and "are made to be." The Word comes to them and they receive it. They *suffer* persecution but maintain the posture of faith. They rejoice in afflictions, but with a joy that is given by the Holy Spirit. Thus they are "imitators," but in a sense they are also "imitations," made like others in the same pattern.

Those "others," in verse 6, are "us," that is, Paul and his fellow missionaries. This could be an "editorial we," but the association of Silvanus and Timothy in the address (1 Thess. 1:1) and the fact that those fellow-workers had also experienced hostility makes it logical to take this as a true plural.[18]

In the related passage, 2:13–14, the same circumstances (reception of the Word and suffering of persecution from their countrymen) mean that the Thessalonians were "made to be like" "the assemblies (churches) of God which are in Judea in Christ Jesus." This illustrates the principle that one must enter the kingdom of God through many tribulations (Acts 14:22) and suffer for the kingdom (2 Thess. 1:5). The Thessalonians' conforming to this pattern is one of the evidences, for Paul, of the genuineness of their election (1 Thess. 1:4).[19]

What does it mean that they became "imitators of the Lord"? The notion that Paul has tacked onto this sentence a self-correcting afterthought can be dismissed.[20] Several commentators[21] point to the fact that the Thessalonians are imitators of the Lord not in "having received the Word" (since Jesus never "came to faith") but only in their having endured affliction and persecution with joy, which the earthly Jesus did according to Hebrews 12:2.[22] Jesus also spoke of the hardships to come upon His disciples and encouraged them to face such tribulations with joy (Matt. 11:12; John 16:33).

Though some knowledge of the life and sayings of the earthly Jesus is certainly presupposed,[23] our vision is probably too limited if we consider this verse to refer merely to the Thessalonians' conscious and active imitation of some specific thing(s) that they knew Jesus had done or said. Paul writes: "imitators . . . of the *Lord*," τοῦ κυρίου, by which he regularly referred to the incarnate, crucified *and risen, glorified and exalted* Jesus.[24] De Boer comments aptly:

Paul's own example of joyous bearing of affliction for the sake of the gospel was of great significance to the Thessalonians. Their personal contact with him had made his example vivid and powerful. But the example of the Lord involved breadths and depths and heights far beyond Paul's. It was the example of a man who had not only faced suffering and death triumphantly, but who had also overcome death itself and had been crowned with everlasting life. He had now reached the destiny for which man was made. The Thessalonians had become imitators of that Lord in the sufferings which they were facing, and they could do so with joy, because they had become sharers in his victory.[25]

This, then, was just one part of that process of their "being conformed" to the image of the Son of God.

Finally, in this they themselves have been made to be a τύπος, a pattern which stands as an example to others in Macedonia and Achaia (1 Thess. 1:7). Paul had noted already with approbation and thanksgiving the results of their faith, the toil (involving extra effort) produced by their love, and the steadfast endurance generated and sustained by their hope (1 Thess. 1:3; cf. Rev. 2:2). All of this, broad in scope, is the work of the power of God in them to transform and renew them from the inside out, to make them imitators of Christ and of God. Paul emphasizes especially and specifically the Thessalonians' joyful steadfastness in the face of persecution as following a pattern imitative of Christ, His apostles, and His churches. In this chain, the life and ministry of Paul, their apostle, has its appropriate place and powerful influence.

B. 2 THESSALONIANS 3:7–9

Paul emphasizes a slightly different aspect of the pattern of the Christ-like life in 2 Thessalonians 3:7–9. Addressing the twin problems of despair and disorderliness that had apparently arisen as a result of a twisting of his teaching about the end of the world,[26] Paul sent a second letter[27] to the new congregation in Thessalonica. He assured them of their destiny as the elect (2 Thess. 2:13–17), and he counseled them to prayer (2 Thess. 3:1–2) and responsible work (2 Thess. 3:6–15) as they await the end of the age with the love of God and the steadfast endurance of Christ in their hearts (2 Thess. 3:5). In the course of his solemn instructions to shun the disorderly,

Paul emphasizes the importance of continuing in the pattern of behavior that they had received as tradition (παράδοσιν, 2 Thess. 3:6) from him.

> For[28] you yourselves know how it is necessary[29] that you imitate[30] us, for we were not [idle and] disorderly[31] among you, nor did we eat bread[32] *gratis* from anyone, but rather [we ate bread] in toil and [extra] effort night and day in order not to impose a burden on any of you; [it was] not that we do not have the right [to eat bread *gratis*],[33] but [we gave up that right] in order to set up ourselves [as] a pattern for you to[34] imitate. (2 Thess. 3:7–9)

This passage shows again the interrelationship of pattern and imitation. But here there is mention only of "us," that is, Paul and his fellow-missionaries. There is no explicit reference to imitation of the Lord.

Nonetheless, the Gospel of Jesus Christ as the power unto salvation and the whole Christian "tradition" stand behind this passage. Paul points to his own behavior as an example for imitation, but he also repeats commands that he had already taught them (2 Thess. 3:10) as Word from God, and refers to "the tradition" the Thessalonians had received from Paul but that he, too, had received (ultimately) from God (3:6). Those commands and this tradition teach the way of life-in-Christ; and Jesus' apostle, Paul, also models it.[35] The Word of the Gospel is the power behind it, for through it God gives the divine gifts of faith, hope, and love. From these spring into being all the fruits of the Spirit.

Here, too, the imitation idea is broad in and of itself. It has to do with "walking in accord with the tradition" (2 Thess. 3:6), that is, Christ-like behavior in all aspects of life. But the specific application of the idea in this passage is narrower. In censuring the lack of respect for order that accompanies an idleness based on false religious notions, Paul points to one aspect of his own behavior as a positive example: his own responsible hard work by which he supported himself during his time in their midst. This self-support was, in his case, an unnecessary "extra effort." It was a work of "supererogation," a walking of the extra mile, for as an apostle he had the right to eat bread *gratis*. But he gave up that right[36] and earned his own bread in order to provide for them an example to imitate, an example of the responsible work that faith produces (cf. 1 Thess. 1:3).

c. 1 Corinthians 4:16

Paul twice uses the imperative form of the verb "to imitate" in 1 Corinthians. The first instance appears in 1 Corinthians 4:16. In countering the factionalism of the Corinthian enthusiasts, Paul needed to deal with the falsely-founded spiritual pride that had bred it. He wrote, therefore, of the proper estimation of the interrelationship of himself, other leaders, and the Corinthian believers (1 Cor. 3:5–4:5). He then says, very pointedly:

> Into this general picture, my friends, I have brought Apollos and myself on your account, so that you may take our case as an example, and learn to "keep within the rules," as they say, and may not be inflated with pride as you patronize one and flout the other.[37]

There follow ironic references to the Corinthians' wealth (1 Cor. 4:8) and a long catalog of the "folly" and "weaknesses" of apostleship (4:9–13). Then, in the context of his special relationship to them as their father in Christ,[38] he appeals: "I beseech you, therefore,[39] [let yourselves be made to] be imitators of me" (1 Cor. 4:16). With the attainment of this goal in mind, Paul says ("therefore," v. 17), he had sent[40] Timothy to them. As a faithful "child" of Paul's, Timothy is a sound imitator of him; in his person and by his words he was to be a "refresher course" in "my ways in Christ, as I teach them everywhere in every church" (4:17).

Here again Paul does his ministry not only with words, but with the "object lessons" of himself and even Timothy. The whole pattern, the way of life, what it means in practical terms to be a Christian, is taught everywhere by Paul. (He hands it on as the tradition, 2 Thess. 3:6.) But he also models it.[41] Such modeling is a part of his ministry, and Timothy's as well.[42]

Of course, it is precisely not as a proud, self-made paragon of virtue that Paul says " . . . be imitators of me." Since "it is no longer I who live, but Christ who lives in me" (Gal. 2:20), "Paul's ways" are "in Christ" and so are in Christ's ways.[43] Paul himself is being conformed to the image of the Son of God.

Once again, therefore, the imitation idea is a very broad-ranging concept. It represents the whole pattern of the Christ-like life.[44] But also once again Paul here applies the concept to a more specific goal: that the Corinthians not be inflated with pride but rather walk in the way of humility, in the footsteps of that buffeted and homeless apostle (1 Cor. 4:11) and of Him who emptied Himself and went to the cross (Phil. 2:5–8).

D. 1 CORINTHIANS 11:1

Finally, nearly all of the points noted above are reiterated in 1 Corinthians 11:1. In the attempt to restore Christian love and concern to the relationships of the "knowers" and the "weak" (1 Cor. 8:10), and to prevent the abuse of freedom that results in the giving of offense (1 Cor. 10:23–33), Paul establishes that "'All things are lawful,' but not all things build up" (1 Cor. 10:23b), and enjoins: "Let no one seek his own good, but the good of his neighbor.... So, whether you eat or drink, or whatever you do, do all to the glory of God. Give no offense .... " (1 Cor. 10:24, 31, 32a, RSV).

Throughout this section Paul has been referring to his own conduct in the ministry. He recounted how he gave up his (Scriptural) right to "get his living by the Gospel" in order not to put any obstacle in the way of the Gospel of Christ (1 Cor. 9:4–18). In order to win the more, he became a slave to all (9:19), "all things to all men, that I might by all means save some" (9:22). He recapitulates in 10:33: " ... just as I try to please all men in everything I do, not seeking my own advantage, but that of many, that they may be saved (1 Cor. 10:33, RSV). Whereupon he enjoins the Corinthians: "[Let yourselves be made to] be imitators of me, as I am of Christ" (1 Cor. 11:1).[45]

The "pattern" to be imitated is again very general: giving up one's rights[46] for the sake of the "advantage" of many others. It is a pattern rooted in the love of God manifested in Jesus, who gave Himself up for the sake of others. It is a pattern that Paul models because of the power of God at work in him. It is a pattern brought into the discussion here for the purpose of urging the "extra effort" toil of love (cf. 1 Thess. 1:3): that the "strong" should give up the rights which, in their freedom, they enjoy, in order not to endanger the spiritual well-being of their "weak" brother.

Christ made that love manifest (Rom. 5:8). Paul, in Christ, modeled it. The Corinthians should emulate Paul in that "more excellent way" (1 Cor. 12:31–13:13).

E. SUMMARY

Paul recognized that his apostleship held a special place in a chain of models for behavior and imitation. With Jesus as Savior and example and with Jesus' Spirit as the transforming power at work in the church, Christians are "saints" who are being made new according to the pattern of Christ. The ministry of the apostle plays a key mediating role also in this area of sanctification, both broadly and as regards specific situations. If Jesus is example, then His apostolic representative and imitator is also an example[47] of the "Christlike way of life" and also of what this means for Christian conduct in specific situations.

Law codes cannot adequately capture the "tradition" of how to behave in the new age. "Love" is the summary of the new standard (John 15:12; Rom. 13:9–10; Gal. 5:14). Christ (and Christ in his apostles and saints) discloses the content of love-in-action. It is not so much taught as caught,[48] through personal contact. This requires a living example of the love of God in action; it requires the ministry of a loving Christian.

Paul took on that key mediating role for his converts, for all who would heed his example. As apostle, he represented Jesus also in this "holiness of the new life in Christ" and this "reflection of the glory of God." As an imitating representative, he, through the power of God at work in his ministry, could mediate a vision of the life to which the lives of the sons of God should be conformed. His behavior became a medium of ministry. Specifically, his behavior revealed humility to the Corinthians and encouraged them to the same. To the Thessalonians, his behavior modeled responsible self-supporting work to maintain one's life while still in this world. In both cases, his conduct revealed something about God and His will for His sons, something for others to see and to imitate and to reflect.

As 1 Thessalonians 1:6 makes clear, the reception of the Word is the first step in this process. For the imitation that is to take place is no mechanical, shallow, "monkey see—monkey do" business. Sinful man does not have the power to accomplish it. This imitation is, as the above translations have consistently reflected, a "letting one's self be made to be like" the Christ who is in Paul. The power for accomplishing this is the Holy Spirit. Into the hearts of those who have received the Word this Spirit is poured out, with the love of God (Rom. 5:5); from this outpouring *grows* the fruit of the Spirit (Gal. 5:22–23). In this way the "new creation," the "one new man in Christ," becomes again what he was meant to be: re-created in the image of God to be the reflection of God's holiness and glory.

All Christians are to be involved in this pattern of imitation and modeling. The apostolic ministry holds a special place of prominence in this process. Apostles are foundational, first-generation keepers and definers of "the tradition." What is true of everybody is true in a heightened sense of an apostle. Hence, even though these verses contain neither the word "mode" nor "imitate," Paul could describe the example-mediating role of himself as apostle in no less comprehensive terms than these:

> Finally, brethren, whatever is true, whatever is honorable, whatever is just, whatever is pure, whatever is lovely, whatever is gracious, if there is any excellence, if there is anything worthy of praise, think about these things. What you have *learned and received and heard and seen in me,* do; and the God of peace will be with you. (Phil. 4:8–9, RSV; emphasis added)

Even after many readings, the boldness of Paul's words continues to surprise. It is a boldness born of the conviction of the power of God at work in his ministry.

3. Paul's Words to His Successors in the Ministry

Paul also made provisions for the continuation of the ministry of the Gospel in his churches when he could not be present in person. He and Barnabas appointed elders in the new congregations of Galatia (Acts 14:23), and he refers to the "overseers and deacons"[49] of the church in Philippi (Phil. 1:1). Elsewhere Paul commends various other individuals in their special roles of service to the Gospel, the Lord, and the church, namely: Silvanus (1 Thess. 1:1), Epaphras (Col. 1:7; 4:12–13), Archippus (Col. 4:17); Tychicus (Eph. 6:21–2): Phoebe (Rom. 16:1–2), Priscilla and Aquila (Rom. 16:3), Andronicus and Junias (Rom. 16:7), Apollos (1 Cor. 3:5–9), as well as other "fellow-workers" and "laborers in the Gospel."[50]

Of course, there are also Timothy, Titus, and the elders at Ephesus. The New Testament records communication from Paul to these workers in the ministry. His words reveal that Paul both held himself up as a model for his assistants and successors in the ministry to imitate and taught them that their behavior, in turn, needed to be exemplary, paradigmatic, reflecting and revealing the holiness of the life of the glorious sons of God.

In his "farewell address" to the Ephesian elders (Acts 20:18–35) Paul reviewed his present perilous situation, charged and warned them, and commended them "to God and to the word of His grace" (v. 32). Then he recalled his practice of earning his own living, having coveted no one's silver or gold. "All these things," he concluded, "I have shown to you, for it is necessary, toiling thus, to aid those who are in need and to remember the words of the Lord Jesus that He himself said: 'It is more blessed to give than to receive'" (Acts 20:35).

More explicitly, the aging apostle gives admonition to Timothy in his "last will and testament":[51] "Follow the pattern of the sound words which you have heard from me, in the faith and love which are in Christ Jesus; guard the truth that has been entrusted to you by the Holy Spirit who dwells within us" (2 Tim. 1:13–14, RSV).

The example of Paul and the instruction from God through Paul's life and ministry are similarly fused in 2 Timothy 3:10–17. Timothy had observed Paul's persecutions and the Lord's rescue (vv. 10–11). There was a lesson in them for him (vv. 12–13). Timothy should: " . . . continue in what you learned and have firmly believed, knowing from whom you learned it and how from childhood you have been acquainted with the sacred writings which are able to instruct you for salvation through faith in Christ Jesus" (2 Tim. 3:14–15, RSV).

Certainly, he learned from Paul, but really he learned from God, God the Holy Spirit "in us" and God the author of sacred Scripture. What he learned from God through Paul corresponded to what God testified to in the inspired Scriptures. Paul's life and Paul's teaching are both a God-sent lesson, a Christ-like paradigm and a Christ-centered tradition for Timothy.

Paul did not intend for this chain of imitation and modeling to end with his departure. To his appointed successors he wrote of how the life and conduct of those set aside in the office of the ministry needs to be an exemplary[52] reflection of the holiness to which all are called in Christ. One can best understand Paul's words in 1 Timothy 3:1-3 and Titus 1:5-9 in this context; they describe a ministry that involves a modeling of the Christ-like life.

These paragraphs are not comprehensive catalogs of qualifications, but broad characterizations of prominent features of the pattern of life that reflects the holiness, the glory, and the love of God. To Timothy and Titus and to the assistants and successors in the ministry whom they shall appoint, Paul says, hold "firm to the sure word as taught" (Titus 1:9; cf. 1 Tim. 3:9). Preservation of the verbal content of the Gospel is a high priority. Equally important is the *conduct* of the candidate for the office of the ministry: in it is preserved the concrete model of the love of God in action.

These paragraphs, therefore, are not legislation; they are an attempt to comprehend a pattern. In giving them Paul reiterates the principle of the model-mediating nature of the conduct of the pastor. These words say, in effect: "You too, Timothy and Titus and all you whom they shall appoint to these offices in the office of the ministry, be imitators of Christ. Be such revealers and reflectors of His holiness and glory and love that you can say (under God, in Christ) to the Christians committed to your care: 'Be *ye* imitators of *me*, as I am of Christ.'"

This calls for a candidate who is "above reproach." His conduct may not be a subject of gossip; rather, there should be a broad consensus that he is indeed a man of godly integrity and love. Paul meant for the great chain of imitation to continue, and for those who serve in his wake in the holy ministry to continue to play a prominent role in modeling what it means to be conformed to the image of the Son of God.

C. Double Standard or Extra Mile?

The premise of this entire book is that those appointed to the office of the ministry today do well to discern and imitate certain patterns in Paul's ministry. This chapter points to this paradigm in Paul: he set his own *conduct* up as an example for others. Those who serve in the ministry, as well as those who certify and supervise them, must realize with utmost seriousness that the pastor's entire life is a medium of his ministry.

This is not to say, of course, that a pastor must be—or maintain the appearance of being—sinless. Paul counted himself "chief" of sinners (1 Tim. 1:15, KJV) and was an illustration of God's love also by being a model recipient of grace (also as "chief," 1 Tim. 1:16).[53] The pastor is surely exemplary in (not exempt from!) living *under* the Word, the Word of judgment and of grace. In this area of justification, all are equal; there is no distinction. "For God locked *all* into disobedience, in order that He might be merciful to *all*" (Rom. 11:32).

However, it is not acceptable to say: "Everyone is a sinner, and so it doesn't matter how a pastor behaves. Since no one can expect to be perfect, anyone can become a pastor, regardless of his conduct." It *does* matter. For when it comes to sanctification, to a testimony to the holiness of God and a reflection of the glory of the life of the sons of God, a higher standard of conduct for the pastor is not merely desirable but *necessary* if the ministry today is to fulfill this New Testament paradigm.[54]

Does a man have to be morally perfect in order to serve in the ministry? No.[55] Men make up the ministry, sinful men whom God is declaring holy and whom the Holy Spirit is in the process of sanctifying. But should those who serve in the ministry be "better," more Christ-like than the rest in their behavior? Yes. They must be enough better to be "above reproach," beyond criticism, not a subject of scandal or gossip—indeed, enough better to earn respect in the eyes of men.

Does this mean operating with a "double standard," a different set of criteria to which pastors must "measure up"? Yes and no. The same Christ is example to all, and the same paradigm of holiness and love is the goal for all. Nor is it really a matter of a "standard" that one must "live up to," but rather of a "pattern" that one will "grow in to." Nevertheless, in human eyes the answer may have to be "yes." For we must make, as well as we are able, evaluations of human conduct *because,* in God's economy, the conduct of the pastor is paradigmatic of the life of Christ. Also, the consequences of the behavior of these men—whether they succeed or fail—are so far-reaching for the spiritual lives of others.

For the sake of the Gospel and its results in the lives of the elect, the life of the minister of the Gospel needs to be "above reproach." As one who testifies to the holiness of God, the pastor testifies also by his own high level of sanctification (his "holiness" in the Holy Spirit) as he draws near to God and handles the divine gifts.[56] As one who preaches the love of God in Christ to others, the pastor also portrays that love in his self-sacrifice for others' benefit. As one who urges others to cultivate the fruit of the Spirit in their lives, the pastor shows what "love, joy, peace, patience, kindness, goodness, faithfulness, gentleness, self-control" (Gal. 5:22–23) entail in daily living.

Sadly, almost every Christian can probably recount the way in which the scandalous behavior of some pastor has hurt the faith of the "little ones."[57] But almost every Christian can also probably point with warm affection to some "saintly" pastor whose life exemplified Christ's love and the fruit of the Spirit. Needless to say, the church needs less of the former and more of the latter. It needs pastors who know it is not adequate to keep repeating: "Do as I say and not as I do." Actions do speak louder than words. Today it also needs pastors who can humbly and sincerely say: "Be imitators of me, even as I am of Christ."

To him who is in Christ, this challenging aspect of the ministry is not so much a chafing requirement or a double standard as it is an opportunity to grow more Christ-like and to walk the extra mile.

Chapter 7

Under the Word of Truth

A. Authority from on High

The determining power and the content of the ministry is the Word of God. It always has been. A word of judgment and promise, it was first spoken by none other than God Himself. When this judgment was reiterated and this promise was repeated, it was repeated as the Word of God entrusted to—indeed, descending upon and invading—human beings.

Never has a human bearer of this message had independent status and authority. The authority of the message he carried has always resided in the fact that he spoke a word from God. The curse against the enemy and the promise of life came into being at the same time, and all of history ever since has been a war of death and life, falsehood and truth,[1] the Word of God against the perversion of it into lies and deceit.

1. Prophets, Priests, and Kings Under the Word

No human institution or lineage could monopolize the Word of God or become the guarantor of its truth. It is always the other way around. Never did the person or the status of the prophet legitimize the word that he spoke. The office of the prophet, or of the king or priest, does not have its own authority (ἐξουσία) but rather has authority *only* insofar as it is in service to the Word of God.

The Old Testament tells of many prophets to whom the Word of the Lord came. They were true prophets, under the control of the Spirit of God. There were false prophets as well,[2] and also the strange (and very instructive) phenomenon of Balaam (Num. 22:1–24:25). Balaam had been conscripted to go and curse the people

84

from whom the promised Savior would come. Yet he is enough of a prophet to know his limitations. He cannot "bless" or "curse." The Word of God does that. Even though, humanly, he may wish to, Balaam *cannot* curse what God has blessed (Num. 23:8). The Word rules him, not vice versa. Similarly, Jeremiah confesses that the Word of the Lord prevails over him, burns within him, and *must* be spoken—even though he may wish not to speak it (Jer. 20:7–10). False prophets speak out of the fear of men and tell men what they wish to hear. But every hearer of the truth knows of the power of the truth when he hears it; and every prophet of the Lord knows why he prophesies and what makes him a prophet:

> The lion hath roared,
> Who will not fear?
> The Lord God hath spoken,
> Who can but prophesy? (Amos 3:8, KJV)

The power and the truth are always in the content of the message, not the status of the person delivering it.

The Old Testament also tells of the priesthood under the Word of the Lord. Some are remembered as faithful priests who carried out their service in accord with God's commands and were zealous for His will (e.g., Aaron, Phineas, and Joshua). Others were disobedient (Nadab and Abihu), negligent (Eli), self-serving (see Jer. 5:31), currying the favor of men (Mal. 1:6–2:9). These come under the Word, the Word of judgment. The person of the priest, in his human intention and action, could in no way be a guarantor of authoritative teaching. It is the height of irony that the high priest in Jesus' day speaks a word of true prophecy about Jesus—but says it only because *he* meant to say the exact opposite (John 11:50; cf. vv. 51 52). The priesthood also testified to the holiness of God and to the plan of salvation only by being obedient to the Word, under the power of the Word. When it departed from such obedience, the Word itself, through another bearer, came to judge it.

The Old Testament describes the kings of Israel, the Lord's anointed ones, in a similar way. Saul was called, chosen, set aside—and rejected. Even David, the man after the Lord's own heart, is not above but under the Word. He, personally, in his status and position, was no authoritative oracle, sole guarantor on earth of the Word of God. He is no self-sufficient religious phenomenon *a la* "Judge

Rutherford" or Jim Jones. He is not immune from the need for reproof. He comes under the Word. The prophet Nathan, bearer of the Word, reproved none less than the Lord's anointed. God sent one bearer of the Word to reprove another in a matter in which the latter, David, was not serving this Word (2 Sam. 12:1–15). In the same vein Isaiah, Jeremiah, and Ezekiel, as prophets, spoke words of warning and judgment upon the kings and leaders of Israel; one bearer of the Word was sent to reprove another. No one man is the measure of the truth.

2. The Word Incarnate

No one man is the measure of the truth—except for the true God and true man, Jesus. He was the fulfillment and the content of the promise; He was the Word incarnate, the Truth itself (John 14:6). He spoke from God, and He taught with *authority*. He alone was the measure of all ministry and all truth.

His authority stood out over against the lack of authority of the religious leaders who supposed themselves to be in a position to pass judgment on Him (cf. Mark 1:27; 2:1–12; Matt. 7:28–9). He amazed them (Luke 2:46–47). He rebuked them (Matt. 23:1–36) and wept over those whom they misled (Matt. 23:37–39). He refuted them and silenced them (Matt. 22:41–46). He reproved them for missing the heart of the matter of the Word of God (John 5:39–40) while setting themselves up as supposed religious authorities (see John 2:18–22; 5:10, 18). Had they been servants of the Word of Truth, the promise, they would have believed in Him who was the fulfillment of the promise; but their own dim glory blinded them.

As He called disciples and set aside apostles, He gave them instruction regarding the nature of their "status" and "authority" (see Mark 10:35–45). He taught them that it was not "membership" in "the twelve" that was important, but a connection to the power that is in the name of Jesus (Mark 9:38–40). He said: "If ye continue in My Word, then are ye My disciples indeed; and ye shall know the truth, and the truth shall make you free" (John 8:31–32, KJV); and He prayed that they should be kept and sanctified through the Word of Truth (John 17:14–17).

3. Apostolic Authority as Ministry Under the Word

To continue that ministry of Jesus in the days after His ascension was precisely the task of every apostle. Each of them testifies that it is nothing but the power of Jesus, working through the Holy Spirit, that empowers his service to the Word. Each of them taught the need to preserve and be preserved in the *truth* of the Gospel, and the need to beware of those who twist and pervert it or who introduce novelties.

Thus St. Luke records the genesis of all apostolic preaching and ministry in the power of the Holy Spirit, descending on Pentecost, as promised by Jesus (Acts 2:1–4; 1:8). St. Peter, apostle of Jesus Christ (1 Peter 1:1), wrote: " . . . if any man minister, let him do it as of the ability which God giveth" (1 Peter 5:11; cf. v. 10). He also gave extensive warning against false prophets (2 Peter 2:1–22) who have their "idiosyncratic" interpretation of Scripture (2 Peter 1:20) and who twist the Scriptures (including Paul's epistles) "unto their own destruction" (2 Peter 3:16). The epistles of John likewise passionately plead for faithfulness to that which was heard "from the beginning" (1 John 1:1; 2:24) over against the lies of those "progressives" (2 John 9) who "went out from us" but are not "of us" (1 John 2:18–26; cf. 2 John 7–11). This "elder" has "no greater joy than to hear that my children walk in truth" (3 John 4). Jude likewise writes to "exhort you that ye should earnestly contend for the faith which was once delivered unto the saints" (Jude 3). Each of them knows that his ministry is under the criterion of the Word of Truth, the "faith" handed down from the "beginning," and that each generation must guard against perversions and novelties. Similarly, the anonymous author of Hebrews, to whom the word of salvation first spoken by the Lord was confirmed "by those who heard Him" (Heb. 2:3), wrote:

> Remember your leaders, those who spoke to you the word of God; consider the outcome of their life, and imitate their faith. Jesus Christ is the same yesterday and today and for ever. Do not be led away by diverse and strange teachings. (Heb. 13:7–9a, RSV)

Apostolic ministry and that which follows it includes responsibility for preservation of the truth and purity of the faith. It is ministry created by the power of the Word, carried out under the criterion of the Word of Truth, and aimed at preserving the life and faith of the believers in the truth of the Word.

B. Apostolic Authority and the Truth of the Gospel in Paul

As one would expect, St. Paul upholds this same truth. He, too, was concerned for the *authentic* authority of the ministry. He knew that his apostleship was not an institutionalized office reflecting the structures of this world, but rather a charism, a gift of gracious power of the new age. He was concerned that the ministry continue as service to that powerful Word, which gives the life and gifts of the new age, and that the ministry not become ossified or perverted through adulterations from false teachers.

1. Words and Deeds

As we have already noted,[3] Paul appointed elders and gave them admonition. He encouraged Timothy and Titus to guard their ministry by faithfulness to the Word of Truth and by vigilance against false doctrine,[4] even as he had earlier encouraged the Roman Christians to beware of those who create divisions and dissension (Rom. 16:17–20).

It is important to recognize that by these appointments and admonitions Paul is not setting up the apostolate, episcopate, priesthood, or diaconate as an institution, which can then become the guarantor of the truth of the Gospel.[5] No human messenger validates, authenticates, or legitimizes the message; the message validates, authenticates, and legitimizes the messenger.[6] Paul makes this clear in a number of passages.

Despite a puzzling paucity of direct quotations from Jesus in his letters, Paul is well-acquainted with the tradition of the sayings and teachings of Jesus. In 1 Corinthians 11:23–25 he quotes Jesus' words of institution as an authoritative, *norming* tradition that has been handed down to and through him. His apostolic injunction must be in accord with it. Likewise in 1 Corinthians 15:3–7 he refers to a formulation describing the death, resurrection, and appearances of Christ. This too is authoritative tradition, the word that norms his preaching and teaching. The normative character of the Old Testament Scriptures, *as they testify to the promise fulfilled in Jesus Christ,* so permeates his letters as to scarcely need mention.[7] The Old Testament is the Word of Truth, and what he preaches and teaches cannot be divergent from its true meaning.[8]

This "Word" and "tradition" are not inert tools, possessions for believers or preachers to use as a resource or a convenient summary of widely held tenets. The Word and tradition are alive and powerful; they take possession of the believers, and they norm and direct the ministers. This Word and tradition is the Gospel itself, the power of God unto salvation for everyone who believes. It is not something the Christians of any generation, not even the apostles', are able to norm and control;[9] rather, it norms them—all of them. It is not at their disposal. They are at its disposal, as Paul intimates in a remarkable phrase that comes up in a somewhat offhand manner in Romans 6:17: "But thanks be to God, that you who were once slaves of sin have become obedient from the heart to the standard of teaching to which you were committed . . . ."[10]

One might think it more likely that Paul would exhort them to live by the tradition *committed to them,* as though it were a resource given to them by which to measure truth and falsehood. There is, of course, some truth to this, and there are passages where Paul does such a thing. But there is more. This tradition, delivered to us and through us, this doctrine is like no other. It is a Word from God and so it is now full of power. It possesses us. We are committed to it, and we are in its hold.[11]

In Paul's day this meant the Gospel as in the Old Testament (rightly interpreted) and in the tradition of the words and deeds of Jesus. In our day it means the Gospel as in the canonical Scriptures of the Old and New Testaments. These have authenticated themselves, in their *autopistia,* as witnesses to the Gospel of Jesus Christ crucified and so have impressed themselves upon Christians and been accepted by the church as the authoritative Word of God. Even as we do not so much "keep the faith" as are "kept in it," so also it is not so much that we must "defend" the Word of God as be kept and defended by it.[12]

Paul knows that he has no right to claim that everything he says must be true simply because of who he is. Rather, he invites *all* teaching and practice to be normed and measured by the Gospel, the powerful Word of God to which *all* have been committed.

2. The Criterion of the Gospel—Applied to Himself and to Others

Paul put his principle into action. We find him not only saying it but doing it, namely, subjecting his own work and that of others to the criterion of the Gospel. It is especially in Galatians that Paul depicts both aspects most graphically. This is not surprising, for it is in Galatians that the two issues of apostolic authority and the truth of the Gospel come together most intimately.

In the opening volley of this epistle Paul makes it clear that he is writing because the truth of *the* Gospel itself—the *one* piece of truly Good News for this world—is at stake: "I am astonished that you are so quickly deserting Him who called you in the grace of Christ and turning to a different gospel—not that there is another gospel .... " (1:6–7a, RSV). Then he makes two solemn anathemas in the form of conditional sentences. The first one is a potential condition: "But even if we, or an angel from heaven, should preach to you a gospel contrary to that which we preached to you, let him be accursed" (1:8, RSV). This is followed by a similar anathema, but in the form of a present general condition, in verse 9: what would be applicable if what is described in verse 8 should happen, is also applicable if *anyone* is now doing it: "As we have previously said I also say again now: if anyone is preaching good news to you contrary to what you received, let him be accursed" (Gal. 1:9).

Two things stand out. First, for all of his insistence that his apostleship is directly from God (Gal. 1:1) and that the content of what he preached was in no way determined or dictated by any of the other apostles (1:11, 15–17), Paul does *not* simply argue that because he is Paul and a true apostle one can therefore believe that what he says is the Gospel truth. The form of the condition in verse 8 neither hints nor denies that Paul (or an angel) is preaching a different, perverted Gospel. The form of the condition simply allows that it *is* a possibility, and that, if it *should* happen, then let Paul or that angel be declared cut off. The form, name, qualifications, or credentials of the messenger cannot stand as a guarantee of the truthfulness of whatever he says.[13] It is not that one can recognize the true Gospel because it is what is taught by an *apostle;* rather, one will be able to discern the difference between "apostolic" and "false" by submitting a teaching to the test of the Gospel.

Second, Paul is confident and insistent that his preaching to the Galatians was faithful to the tradition of the true Gospel. "What we preached to you," "that which you received," namely: Jesus Christ crucified, received through faith (Gal. 3:1–2) *is* the *true* Gospel. This is attested by the accompanying reception of the Spirit, miracles, and freedom (Gal. 3:5; 4:7, 31), and it is in accord with the Word of God of the Old Testament, rightly understood (Gal. 3:6–14; 4:21–31). While he did not receive this Gospel from any human source, Paul does recount that those who were with Jesus "beginning from the baptism of John until the day when he was taken up" (Acts 1:22) did attest, with the hand of fellowship, that Paul was preaching the same Gospel as they had received from the Lord Jesus and His Spirit (Gal. 2:7–9).

Paul walks a fine line in Galatians 1 and 2. He defends himself against attacks by arguing that the Gospel he preached is the truth of the God of the Old Testament, of the Lord Jesus Christ, and of the Holy Spirit. This is his center, his criterion, and the offhand illustrative condition in 1:8 shows clearly that he is ready to have his own preaching and ministry evaluated on the basis of it.

Yet he cannot stop there. The preaching and practice of others must also be submitted to the same test. It is a matter of the truth of the Gospel. Galatians also affords a dramatic example of Paul's sense of responsibility for ministry in accord with the truth of the Gospel. He reports his confrontation with Cephas, Gal. 2:11–14:[14]

> But[15] when Cephas[16] came to Antioch, I opposed him face to face[17] because he stood condemned.[18] For before certain ones from James came[19] he customarily ate with the Gentiles, but when they came, he withdrew and kept himself separate, fearing those of the circumcision. And the rest of the Jews joined him in behaving inconsistently, so that even Barnabas[20] was carried away by their hypocrisy. But when I saw that they were not behaving correctly with respect to the truth of the Gospel, I said to Cephas before them all: "If you, being a Jew, live in the life-style of a Gentile and not of a Jew, how do you compel the Gentiles to live in the life-style of Jews?[21]

Clearly, Paul is reproving not only Peter but any and all others who advocate or who are carried away into behavior indicative of the doctrine of the Judaizers. Peter's behavior is illustrative. It may also have had considerable impact due to his position or reputation in the early church. As an apostle whom others were to "imitate," his inconsistency in behavior had greater consequences. The cause of the truth of the Gospel requires that every undermining of the Gospel be opposed (Gal. 2:1–5, as well as the situations in Corinth and Colossae), but here it was a matter of needing to give public reproof to a fellow-apostle. For the sake of the truth of the Gospel, Paul was ready to undertake the delicate, even dirty business of opposing a fellow-apostle, face to face and in public, on the matter of behavior that was not consistent with the Gospel.

Paul's actions applied his principle that the messenger is under the Word and is judged by the Word. Not only is he prepared to submit his own ministry to that standard, he is ready to criticize others on the basis of that same criterion. He is responsible to the Lord for truthfulness and genuineness in the ministry. The personal prestige of the individual involved does not matter (cf. Gal. 2:2, 6, 9; 5:10); the truth of the Gospel rules over the ministry.[22] Paul was as bold as he needed to be; nevertheless, being skilled at the proper application of Law and Gospel, he was ready to change his tone of voice (cf. Gal. 4:7; 2 Cor. 7:8–13) to be as gentle as he could be (cf. 1 Thess. 2:7; Gal. 6:1).

3. A Paradigm of Responsibility

Paul also provides a paradigm of yet another sort. It is the paradigm of a relationship not between those set aside for the ministry and those committed to their care, but a relationship among those in the ministry. Under the Word, Paul is responsible to the Word; as a member of the "ministerium," the sum total of the individuals set aside into the office of the ministry, he has a responsibility that all ministry be carried out under the Word. He has a responsibility for the authenticity, under the Word, of the Gospel ministry of the ministerium as a whole.

The ultimate goal is the spiritual health of the church and of those laypersons committed to the care of the ministerium. This concern is also expressed through a readiness to evaluate and reprove the teachings and the actions of any given individual—himself or another—in the ministry. This evaluation is done on the basis of the truth of the Gospel—and nothing else.[23]

C. Being Truthful in Love in the Ministry

Each person in the ministry is responsible to his Lord, who has entrusted him with the stewardship of these mysteries and treasures. He is responsible to those entrusted to his care—to offer them, in accord with Christ's will, Gospel ministry. He is also responsible to ensure that the ministerium, all those individual men in the ministry, are providing pure Gospel ministry to the church. This means that pastors, under the Word and in the divine doctrine, may need to become bearers of the Word who speak reproof to another bearer of the Word who is not serving the Word in some particular matter. This is what Nathan, Malachi, and Paul were doing—all in the pattern of Jesus himself. It is what Martin Luther undertook to do in posting his 95 theses and in his many other writings. It is what all who set out to institute reforms in the ministry of the church have meant to do, and the justification of their actions lies in the extent to which they accomplished restoration of Gospel ministry under the Word. Men in the ministry today need to accept this responsibility as well.

As Paul was able to be bold or gentle, so men in the ministry today shall need to be bold and gentle among their peers. They may need the godly boldness that is no respecter of persons or of reputations. The authority of the ministry is always and only the authority of the Word of God; there is no position in the ministry that is exempt from evaluation and reproof under that criterion. Each person serving in the ministry must be ready to let his words and deeds—his life—be subjected to scrutiny and evaluation, not on the basis of human criteria,[24] but by that standard of teaching to which we have all been committed, specifically, the truth of the Gospel.

Any person in the ministry who replaces the authority of the Word of God with an authority of human status, or who is exceeding the bounds of or perverting the shape of his Gospel commission and charge,[25] must be reproved—no matter who he is or may appear to be. It must be done, for the sake of the Gospel, the ministry, and the church.

In more "worldly" terms, the ministerium today needs to be a better "self-policing" profession.[26] It is not a "profession" of "independent operators." Neither "congregational autonomy" nor the twisting of the doctrine of the "call" into the ministry into something

93

like permanent and unimpeachable tenure can ever justify a claim to be exempt from the responsibility to evaluate and reprove, and to be evaluated and reproved, by the standard of the Gospel. No dukes in their fiefdoms may continue in unchallenged autocracy in their own bailiwicks.

The ministerium as a total entity is greater than any one individual. (Even Paul knew that no congregation was served by one and only one minister, cf. 1 Cor. 3:5–10.) Each needs to see his work in the perspective of the larger picture, and to evaluate his own work by the Gospel—and eagerly to expect his peers' assistance in such evaluation. Each needs to be ready to participate in the evaluation (and evaluation does not always result in total approbation) of the work of another.

It should *never* come to the point where a Christian congregation has to remove its pastor from the office of the ministry.[27] The aid and counsel of his close peers and supervisors in the ministry should first succeed in reproving and correcting an erring brother and/or in confirming him in the rightness of his position in the eyes of those whom he has been sent to serve. Paul's encouragements to such as Timothy and Titus as well as his reproof of Peter can provide a paradigm also for this important aspect of ministry under the Word.

To be sure, this is a dangerous business. Human beings, even sanctified ones, do not always take reproof well.[28] Human beings, even sanctified ones, do not always undertake to evaluate and to reprove in a manner that does not "consider anyone from a human point of view" (cf. 2 Cor. 5:16). Consequently, it is of the utmost importance to heed Paul's words in Galatians: "Brethren, if a man is overtaken in any trespass, you who are spiritual should restore him in a spirit of gentleness. Look to yourself, lest you too be tempted" (Gal. 6:1, RSV).[29] If the boldness that is required is the boldness to speak and stand up for the truth of the Gospel, then the gentleness is the same as love. Ephesians 4:15 has captured it:[30] "being truthful in love."

Loving the Lord, loving his people, and loving our brothers in the ministry means that we *are* "our brother's keeper."[31]

Chapter 8

A Partnership in Joy

A. Getting Things in Perspective

The man whom God created He also installed as the steward and overseer of His garden (Gen. 2:15). In Eden, Adam's duty was his delight; all that he needed for a happy life was his, as he obeyed (Gen. 2:16). Work was not burdensome. He and Eve could be as carefree as the lilies of the field.

But the steward and his helpmeet lost their post, and they were expelled from Eden. Pain came on the scene; and work, under the curse of sin, became ugly toil (Gen. 3:16–19; cf. 6:29). Worry grew up in that soil of distrust. Competition, greed, hatred, and more misery came into the world (Gen. 4:3–11). Humanity now had to wander through a world that gave its goods to him only grudgingly (Gen. 4:12). In the sweat of his brow did he eat his bread. The paradise he had lost was nothing but a memory—and a promise and a hope.

It was and is a frustrating situation. Men and women need the life-sustaining fruits of the physical creation and must work to receive them. (Even then, they only receive them under God's blessed sun, rain, and growth.) But they must learn neither to worry over them nor to hoard them, for their ultimate goal is life with God forever in paradise restored, where there is no pain, no toil, no worry, no want.

1. The Pilgrim People and This World's Goods

Abraham, the son of the wandering Aramean, lived in the "promised land" in tents, as a sojourner, looking for the city God would build (cf. Heb. 11:9–10). God fed His people, as they wandered in the desert, with "daily" bread (which they could neither sell nor hoard, Ex. 16:14–36). At the same time, He also told them, "man doth not live by bread only, but by every word that proceedeth out of the mouth of the Lord doth man live" (Deut. 8:3, KJV). The Lord's prophets pointed to the dangerous temptation of preoccupation with this world's wealth (e.g., Amos 4:1–3; 6:1–8), and they pointed forward to the joy of life together in communion with God (Is. 35:1–10, a vision of paradise restored). One wealthy and wise man wrote of the vanity of all toil and pleasures under the sun (Eccl. 1:12–2:11), while another showed how to keep the Giver and not the gifts of life in sharp focus: "The Lord gave, and the Lord hath taken away; blessed be the name of the Lord" (Job 1:21, KJV).

2. The Visitor from Beyond the Sun

When Jesus came, He was born in a manger, and not to be found among the rulers and the wealthy of this world. "The foxes have holes, and the birds of the air have nests," He said, "but the Son of Man hath not where to lay His head" (Matt. 8:20, KJV). As to the necessities of this life, He allowed that He (and His disciples) be supported out of the substance of "those who had" (Luke 8:1–3). On the day of His triumph He rode another's donkey (Mark 11:1–6). In His time of trial He took His meal in another's guest room (Mark 14:12–16). Upon His death He was laid in another's grave (Matt. 27:57–60).

But He was the visitor from beyond the sun, the "dayspring from on high" (Luke 1:78). He came to give the greatest treasure (Matt. 13:44–46), the one thing needful (Luke 10:42): victory over the world (John 16:33) and a room in the heavenly mansion (John 14:2–3).

It is not that He was against money and such. More specifically, He attributed so little value to them in relation to the value of doing God's will to accomplish the plan of salvation. Pay the temple tax, he said (even though "the sons" are free); God will provide the way (Matt. 17:24–27). Render to Caesar Caesar's silly coins (Matt. 22:15–22). Let not mammon be your master (Matt. 6:24), "but seek ye first the kingdom of God, and His righteousness; and all these things shall be added unto you" (Matt. 6:33, KJV). "Lay not up for yourselves treasures on earth," He said, for He knew that "where your treasure is, there will your heart also be" (Matt. 5:19, 21, KJV).

96

He also instructed his apostles: "You received without pay, give without pay. Take no gold, nor silver, nor copper in your belts, no bag for your journey, nor two tunics, nor sandals, nor a staff; for the laborer deserves his food."[1] As messengers of a Gospel from the world above calling men to the promised life of the world above, they were to demonstrate (as did Israel in the desert) the "other-worldly" character of their calling through the manner in which they handled the business of the necessities of life in this world.

3. Sojourners, Seeking a Better Homeland

The apostles lived and wrote in the pattern of all the faithful, acknowledging that they are "strangers and exiles" "seeking a homeland," "a better country, that is, a heavenly one" (Heb. 11:13–16). James delivered a scathing denunciation of the value of worldly wealth and the ways some men had amassed it (James 5:1–6), and he also warned all Christians against tailoring their behavior in accord with the tailoring of him with whom they deal (James 2:1–7). St. Peter contrasted the inheritance kept in heaven, which is imperishable, with gold or silver, which though precious are perishable (1 Peter 1:4, 7, 18; cf. vv. 23–25 and 5:4). St. John explicitly encouraged continuation of the system whereby Christian teachers and missionaries are supported, in this life's needs, by the hospitality of those to whom they minister (3 John 5–8, cf. vv. 10, 12; and 2 John 10–11). In all of this these apostles followed the model established by Jesus; they provide an object lesson of the transitoriness of this world's goods and the need to focus on the treasure of the joy of the world to come.

B. Preachers and Money According to St. Paul

Also on this matter St. Paul is of one accord with the Biblical tradition, with Jesus and the other apostles. His estimation of this world's goods, combined with His special, unique personal way of fulfilling his Gospel ministry, provides yet one more paradigm of relationship: a partnership in joy.

1. General Principles

Paul also taught all Christians that their citizenship is in heaven (Phil. 3:20) and that they should therefore keep their relationship to this world's riches in proper perspective. Being a Christian means that the world is crucified to a person, and vice versa (Gal. 6:14). It means putting on Christ and putting off covetousness (Col. 3:5). The wealthy of this world should not "set their hopes on uncertain riches, but on God who richly furnishes us with everything to enjoy," and they are to be "rich in good deeds," to "take hold of the life which is life indeed" (1 Tim. 6:17–19, RSV). To all he encouraged generosity, a sharing of the goods of this world with the less fortunate (cf. Acts 20:35; Eph. 4:28). This is especially evident in the gathering of the collection for the poor fellow Christians in Jerusalem (cf. 2 Cor. 8:1–9:15, esp. 8:14). But he rebuked those who acted as though being a Christian meant paying no heed whatsoever to the orderly conduct of the business by which the life of this age is sustained (2 Thess. 3:6–13; cf. Rom. 13:6–7).

As regards specifically those who serve in the ministry, he gave strong warning not to imagine that "godliness is a means of gain" (1 Tim. 6:5). For "those who desire to be rich fall into temptation, into a snare, into many senseless and hurtful desires that plunge men into ruin and destruction. For the love of money is the root of all evils . . . . " (1 Tim. 6:9–10a, RSV). He laid down the guidelines for all who aspire to the office of the ministry that they be "no lover of money" (1 Tim. 3:3) and not "greedy for gain" (Titus 1:7). Nonetheless, he also makes it very clear, as a general principle, that those in the ministry have the Scripturally-established right to be supported in the needs of this life by those whom they serve (1 Cor. 9:4–12). "Let him who is taught the word share all good things with him who teaches" (Gal. 6:6, RSV).[2]

Thus Paul also upholds the two necessary parts of the system for preaching the Gospel while living in this present age: provision for the necessities of this life, but concentration on the joys of the life of the age to come.

2. Paul's Exceptional Practice

Interestingly enough, Paul's behavior in this matter is not a crystal clear example of the "letter of the law" of his instructions. For he made it his usual practice to do something exceptional. In 1 Corinthians 9, where he defends the right of those who proclaim the Gospel to get their living by the Gospel, he also explains: "Nevertheless, we have not made use of this right, but we endure anything rather than put an obstacle in the way of the gospel of Christ" (1 Cor. 9:12b, RSV).

For the sake of the Gospel, though free from all men, he made himself a slave to all, in order by all means to save some (1 Cor. 9:19, 22–23). This appears to have been an especially important matter to Paul in Corinth (cf. 1 Cor. 4:12; 2 Cor. 11:7–11) and in Thessalonica (1 Thess. 2:3–10), where Paul insisted upon his absolute integrity with regard to taking money from them.[3] But he also points to it as his practice in Ephesus as well, where he did not covet anybody's silver or gold (Acts 20:33–35). This, however, is a financial sacrifice beyond the call of duty, exceptional behavior in which Paul might "boast" (1 Cor. 9:15). Still, it is behavior that models Jesus' attitude and reflects His instructions to His messengers regarding their attitude towards this world's wealth. All are called to emulate this attitude, even if they are not all *required* to emulate the specific deeds of Paul himself at this point.

3. An Exception to the Exception

In Paul's practice there was one notable and paradigmatic exception. Only with you, he says to the Philippians, did I enter into a partnership of giving and receiving.[4] Here he shows how to be in a relationship with a congregation where money is no problem and joy abounds. He and the Philippians model partnership in the Gospel, partnership in joy.

Paul had his tough cases. But he also had cases like the Philippians. His epistle to them may be his most intensely personal letter. Apart from the brief warnings and admonitions in chapter 3, there appears to have been no other reason for his having written it other than to give his personal response to and reflections upon what Martin Franzmann called "the golden chain of Philippi's gracious generosity."[5] From the very beginning there existed between Paul and the Philippians a commonality, a sharing, a partnership that would abide. Lydia's response to his preaching at the place of prayer and her immediate generosity (Acts 16:13–15) set the tone and led to a sharing of their goods with Paul. This unique relationship continued even into the time of Paul's imprisonment in Rome, when the Philippians sent Epaphroditus to him with more gifts.

Paul refers to this sharing, and to the joy that it has brought him, at several points in his letter. In 4:10, 15 he mentions their former generosity, now revived. In 2:25–29 he tells them what Epaphroditus has meant to him and why he is sending him back—for their joy. In 4:10–19 he speaks of the joy that their gifts had brought to his heart and of his joy that in their generosity there is evidence of "fruit" that will increase to their credit as "God will supply every need" of theirs according to His riches.

From Philippians 4 we can discern why it is that such a joyful sharing of this world's goods can go on. Money is no problem between them because both Paul and the Philippians have it in perspective in relationship to the Gospel. For his part, Paul says:

> Not that I complain of want; for I have learned, in whatever state I am, to be content. I know how to be abased, and I know how to abound; in any and all circumstances I have learned the secret of facing plenty and hunger, abundance and want. I can do all things in Him who strengthens me. (Phil. 4:11–13, RSV)

It is "not that I seek the gift," he says, for "I have received full payment, and more" (Phil. 4,17a, 18a). The Philippians' gifts represent a revival of their concern (φρονεῖν) for him (4:10). They are a fruit that increases to their credit (4:17). They are a "fragrant offering, a sacrifice acceptable and pleasing to God" (4:18). God will respond to them by supplying all they need "according to His riches in glory in Christ Jesus" (4:19). Where such attitudes and faith abound, God is glorified (4:20) and money is never a problem.

This kind of sharing, this partnership and the joy based upon it, are rooted in an even deeper relationship between Paul and his congregation in Philippi. In the exordium[6] of this epistle he sounds the note of the joy-inspiring partnership between himself and the Philippians:

> I thank my God in all my remembrance of you, always in every prayer of mine for you all making my prayer with joy, thankful for your partnership in the gospel from the first day until now. And I am sure that He who began a good work in you will bring it to completion at the day of Jesus Christ. It is right for me to

feel thus about you all, because I hold you in my heart, for you are all partakers with me of grace [συγκοινωνούς μου τῆς χάριτος] both in my imprisonment and in the defense and confirmation of the gospel. (Phil. 1:3–7, RSV)

Paul therefore goes on to say that his imprisonment has contributed of the spreading of the Gospel,[7] and that the Philippians, though separated from him in this activity by hills and seas, have been a part of it through the support of their prayers (Phil. 1:19) as well as their gifts and the sending of Epaphroditus. Furthermore, *their* struggle to live a life worthy of their calling in Philippi is done as a result of *Paul's* preaching and teaching and exhorting and writing and praying for them. So in their life, which also includes suffering, they are engaged in the same struggle as he is: "For it has been granted to you that for the sake of Christ you should not only believe in Him but also suffer for His sake, *engaged in the same conflict* which you saw and now hear to be mine" (Phil. 1:29–30, RSV, emphasis added). They are his partners, and he is theirs.

Therefore, whether Paul should be released or depart, whether it should happen that he come again to them or not, they and he are still "partners," "striving side by side for the faith of the gospel" (1:27). Their sharing goes truly far beyond the sharing of goods and gifts; indeed, the sharing of goods and gifts exists only *because of* this deeper sharing as partners in the Gospel. They shared in the humility that characterizes all recipients of grace. They shared in the self-sacrifice and in the suffering that is part of striving for the faith of the Gospel. They were partners together (συγκοινωνούς) both in suffering and in the defense and confirmation of the Gospel (1:7).

This sense of fellowship and partnership in what was shared led Paul to such expressions of joy as we find in Philippians, joy not just over having received gifts from them, but joy over their standing firm in the faith. Thus he says: "Even if I am to be poured as a libation upon the sacrificial offering of your faith, I am glad and rejoice with you all. Likewise you also should be glad and rejoice with me" (Phil. 2:17–18, RSV).[8]

Whether he lives or dies, he lives with all of those who have received new life in Jesus Christ. Those he leaves behind are still striving and standing firm; they stand fast in the Lord, and he lives.

Partners in the Gospel, they are partners in eternal life. Under such terms, sharing the temporary blessings of this life is very easy and very natural.

C. Partnership in Joy

Application of this paradigm to the present-day relationship of pastors and congregations comes easily. One does not have to look very far or listen very long to learn of horror stories of conflicts between pastors and congregations. Very often these conflicts involve money, the love of which is the root of all evils. There are numerous examples of pastors who are striving to live in the lifestyle of corporation executives. Rumors circulate of lawsuits and countersuits and policies and clauses written to protect against litigation. What has it come to?

Consider the mentality, the love of money, involved when a pastor lets it be known that he could take a call if the salary were higher—or if there were a big interest-free loan offered for a down payment on a house. Consider the potential dangers when church leaders gather and adopt a salary scale and equity-building program for church workers in order to make "church vocations more attractive." Consider the inappropriateness of the young pastor who has a "career plan"[9] to move on from his first (small) parish to something bigger in about two or three years. Consider how far we have come from a partnership in joy when congregation members devise ways to keep money flowing only toward their pet projects rather than toward charities or a more generous support of their pastor.

How much bickering and resentment and even scandal could be avoided if pastors and congregations could have this vision of partnership, communion, oneness in joy in the service of the Gospel? It would be a harmonious testimony to their "upward calling in Christ" if they would live out the consequences of their partnership in the Gospel in a financial relationship characterized by joyful generosity and joyous contentment. A step in the right direction can be made when pastors learn the lesson, the "secret" of which Paul speaks: "in whatever state I am, to be content," and to face "both abundance and want" "in Him who strengthens me" (Phil. 4:11–13). A step in the right direction can be made also when con-

gregations learn to view their monetary gifts to church not just as donations toward an organization's budget, but as "a fragrant offering, a sacrifice acceptable and pleasing to God" (Phil. 4:18).[10]

Jesus and Paul lay before all Christians the invitation to believe in earnest that it *is* "more blessed to give than to receive" (Acts 20:35), that generosity *is* a Christian virtue with its own special kind of return (Phil. 4:17b), and that no one will ever have to do without because of having been generous in sharing and giving such sacrificial offerings, for "my God will supply every need of yours according to His riches in glory in Christ Jesus" (Phil. 4:19). It is hard for money to be a problem where these lessons have been learned.

Paul had his tough cases. Yet he also had congregations like the Philippians. Every pastor has some Philippians: partners, supporters, and a source of joy. They are those who are one with him in Christ, one in the suffering and in the defense and confirmation of the Gospel. They are always "striving side by side" with him (even from afar). They may not always be congregational officers or even big givers; they may be just the quietly present worshipers and helpers in the smaller tasks. They may not be the ones showing him where he should put the furniture in the parsonage, but rather the ones who just sneak up and leave a jug of iced tea on the doorstep on moving day. They know that their pastor is human, but they know that neither he nor they should be worldly, since they know that we are all left to be "in the world, but not of the world" (John 17:15–16). They are a joy, a foretaste of the heavenly commonwealth. The example of the relationship of St. Paul and the Philippians shows us how this partnership in the Gospel is a source of true contentment and abiding joy in doing the work of the holy ministry.

Reclaiming Patterns of Ministry—A Word of Consolation and Encouragement

Much of what has been said in these pages can be read as prescriptions: what we ought to do and not do. That is a definition of "law." No one is saved by it. No holy living is produced by it. It accuses the sinner in every one of us. It accuses and convicts me. May it so accuse and convict any other sinner who reads these pages as well.

But do not let that be the end of the story. Just to express exasperation and produce despair were certainly not the goals of this book. These pages can also be read, and hopefully they will be read, as descriptions: what God would work for the church in and through those set aside into the office of the ministry. Insofar as it be "Law," let it also find application in the "third use" of the Law: guidance for people being sanctified.

Hopefully, we have made a modest contribution toward a better ministerium by having delineated Scriptural patterns in Jesus and Paul. If we have incidents of failure in the ministry, let them be due to human weakness, rather than a failure to have understood from the start what is really involved in the pastoral calling.

Our Lord Jesus told two parables in which He taught the wisdom of "counting the cost" (Luke 14:28–32). Let each one set aside to the ministry, and each one aspiring so to be set aside, let him count the cost: have a clear vision of the nature of the calling. Let those so served give room and support and encouragement to their pastors to fulfill their true ministry.

It is arduous. It is awesome. Frankly, it is frightening, for it is impossible.

It is impossible for a human being. But, as St. Paul reminds us, the new life in Christ is not a matter of "I" but of "Christ in me" (Gal. 2:20). His overflowing power fills earthen vessels and makes them equal to the task of the ministry (2 Cor. 4:7). There is no more positive, optimistic, or encouraging note on which I can close than Paul's own words:

> Not that we are sufficient of ourselves, to consider anything as originating within ourselves, but on the contrary, that which makes us equal to the task originates in God, who indeed did make us be up to it to be ministers of a new covenant, not characterized by "letter" but rather by "Spirit." For "letter" kills, but the Spirit makes alive. (2 Cor. 3:5–6)

In this truth about the ministry there lies a basis for confidence (2 Cor. 3:4).

NOTES

CHAPTER 1

1. There is even disagreement as to whether "the ministry" is an *ordo* of persons, a constellation of functions, or an *officium*, a divine institution administered by specially set-aside men. A survey that documents the variety is David S. Schuller, Merton P. Strommen, and Milo L. Brekke, *Ministry in America* (San Francisco: Harper & Row, 1980). Georg H. Vischer reviewed ecumenical documents over the past 50 years in *Apostolischer Dienst* (Frankfurt am Main: Lembeck, 1982) and, on pp. 202–09, asserts that there are now four basic conceptions of church and ministry: [Roman] Catholic, "denominational," evangelical [Lutheran], and a mediating "ecumenical" view. Other major works illustrating the range of expectation are Donald P. Smith, *Clergy in the Cross Fire* (Philadelphia: Westminster, 1973), S. Hiltner, *Ferment in the Ministry* (Nashville: Abingdon, 1969), and C. R. Fielding, *Education for Ministry* (Dayton: American Association of Theological Schools, 1966).

2. There may also be a tension between what a congregation wants in a minister and what, in God's will, it should have. A classic description of the sources of frustration and a handbook of common sense guidance is William E. Hulme, *Your Pastor's Problems: A Guide for Ministers and Laymen* (Minneapolis: Augsburg, 1966). Two recent books that try to give pastors encouragement and advice in their current plight are E. M. Grider, *Can I Make It One More Year?* (Atlanta: John Knox, 1980), and M. Shelley, *Well-Intentioned Dragons* (Waco: Word, 1985).

3. On the built-in tension of the calling, see chaps. 1–4 of Richard John Neuhaus, *Freedom for Ministry: A Critical Affirmation of the Church and Its Mission* (San Francisco: Harper & Row, 1979).

4. Smalcald Articles, Part III, Art. xii, 2. Translations of the Lutheran Confessions, unless otherwise noted, are from the *The Book of Concord*, trans. and ed. Theodore G. Tappert, *et al.* (Philadelphia: Fortress, 1959).

5. Latin: *officium;* German: *Amt.* Equivalents in the Greek of the New Testament might be οἰκονομία (1 Cor. 9:17; Eph. 3:2; Col. 1:25: "arrangement," "economy," "stewardship") or ἐξουσία (Matt. 10:6; Acts 8:19; Rom. 13:1: "authority," "responsibility").

6. They work *ex opere operato,* in the original and good sense of that term, as used to oppose the Donatist heresy.

7. Earlier attempts, of a different sort from the present one, to extract from the Scriptures materials helpful to the ministry today include E. E. Shelp and R. Sunderland, eds., *A Biblical Basis for Ministry* (Philadelphia: Westminster, 1981), T. J. Mullen, *The Renewal of The Ministry* (Nashville: Abingdon, 1963), and James D. Smart, *The Rebirth of Ministry* (Philadelphia: Westminster, 1960).

8. *New Testament Models for Ministry* (Nashville: Nelson, 1983). The same book is available under the title *New Testament Foundations of Ministry,* Marshall's Theological Library (London: Marshall Morgan & Scott, 1983). Smart, pp. 38–40, drew attention to the lines of continuity running from Jesus to the apostles to the ministry today; he emphasized Jesus' activities in preaching, teaching, and pastoral care, all in the context of His suffering. A careful discussion of the relationship (despite the differences) of the office of the ministry to the apostolate is K. H. Rengstorf, *Apostolate and Ministry,* trans. Paul D. Pahl (St. Louis: Concordia, 1969). Both pastor and apostle are *representative* of Jesus, and under His call, authority, and Word (pp. 45–52). See also Carl E. Braaten, *The Apostolic Imperative* (Minneapolis: Augsburg, 1985), pp. 116–31. In an earlier article, Martin Franzmann combined the two ideas of imitation and authoritative apostolic representation, see *Scripture and Interpretation* (Springfield: Concordia Seminary Print Shop, 1961), pp. 36–49. But much earlier still in the course of his interpretation of Ps. 84:3 (*First Lectures on the Psalms II, 76–126,* ed. Hilton C. Oswald, *Luther's Works,* American Edition, Vol. 11, [St. Louis: Concordia, 1976], pp. 138–44; cf. WA, III, 644–48, where the reference is to Ps. 83:4), Martin Luther showed that he held a similar understanding of the interrelationship of Christ, the apostles, and the clergy; and of the significance of this for Christians. (The fact that his interpretation contains some healthy doses of allegory does not affect the point made here.)

9. Kruse, pp. 13–64. The first large section of this work, on Jesus, is flawed by its use of only the synoptic tradition and by repeated deliberations over the authenticity of any discussed logion, as measured by Kruse's particular manner of applying the "criteria of authenticity."

10. The quotation may be found in the Babylonian Talmud, Ber. 5, 5 (34b), and in further places given in SB, III, 2. An extensive application of *shaliach* to the subject of the Christian apostolate is to be found in K. Rengstorf, "apostellō, k.t.l.," TDNT I, 398–447; see esp. pp. 414–20.

11. See Gal. 1 and 2, and Franzmann, pp. 39–40. That the link to the power of the name of Jesus, rather than any commissioning ceremony or status of apostleship, is what is most important in this "chain" is demonstrated by the remarkable pericope of the "unknown exorcist," Mark 9:38–40; Luke 9:49–50.

12. This is presented in great clarity in T. W. Manson, *The Servant-Messiah* (Grand Rapids: Baker, 1977).

13. See the forceful exposition of Rom. 1:1 along these lines by Martin Luther in his *Lectures on Romans,* ed. Hilton C. Oswald, *Luther's Works,* American Edition, Vol. 25 (St. Louis: Concordia, 1972), pp. 140–41.

CHAPTER 2

1. Martin Franzmann, "O God, O Lord of Heaven and Earth," *Worship Supplement*, authorized by the Commission on Worship, The Lutheran Church—Missouri Synod and Synod of Evangelical Lutheran Churches (St. Louis: Concordia, 1969), No. 758.

2. Compare Amos 5:4; Jer. 21:8.

3. Is. 66:10–13 uses the figure of a *mother* and child. In vv. 10–12 *Jerusalem* is the "mother" from whom the rejoicing saints of the time of salvation are nursed; in v. 13 *God* assures the audience that He will comfort them, "as a man whom his mother comforts." But then the explanatory word is appended: "in [or: by] Jerusalem." One might suggest that God's *compassion (rachamim)* for His people in the Old Testament (e.g., Ps. 102:13; Is. 63:7) is rooted in a "motherly" metaphor, since the root of this word-group (*rchm*) is also the source of *rechem*, "womb" (a state of affairs which is true also in cognate Semitic languages). The derivation is hypothesized (see BDB, s.v.) as from either "brotherly feeling" (as between those born from the same womb) or "motherly feeling." But this would probably be an improper use of etymology. In usage *racham,* etc. do *not* show themselves to belong especially to a mother-child relationship— indeed, compare Ps. 103:13: "As a *father pities* his children . . . ." But Moses' rhetorical questions to God in Num. 11:10–15 do imply a relationship of God and His people under the figure of a mother and child: birth and nursing. Moses says (v. 12): "Was it I who conceived all this people, was it I who gave them birth that you should say to me, 'Carry them in your bosom, like a nurse with a baby at the breast . . . '?" (JB). The implied answer is: "No, it was not you, Moses. It is I, God, who gave them birth and should carry and nurse them." Old Testament descriptions of God's creative work include "birth" metaphors as well as a "begetting" metaphors. Thus in Ps. 90:2, the psalmist describes the creation of the mountains, earth, and world as being the result of both God's begetting (*yld*) and of His giving birth amidst throes (*chul*). In His saving work, correspondingly, God is the subject of metaphorical expressions in relationship to Israel, as in Deut. 32:18: "You were unmindful of the Rock that begot you, and you forgot the God who gave you birth" (RSV).

4. See R. W. Funk, "The Apostolic *Parousia,* Form and Significance," in *Christian History and Interpretation* (John Knox *Festschrift*), ed. W. Farmer, C. F. D. Moule, and R. R. Niebuhr (Cambridge: Cambridge University Press, 1967), p. 249.

5. Martin Franzmann and Walter Roehrs, *Concordia Self-Study Commentary* (St. Louis: Concordia, 1979), p. 142 of "The New Testament," written by Franzmann.

6. The admonition to be "imitators of me" is closely tied to the "spiritual parent-children" language. This is the well-presented thesis of an excellent monograph by Willis Peter de Boer, *The Imitation of Paul* (Kampen: J. H. Kok, 1962), see esp. p. 214. The thought is also found in Gal. 4:12, in the same context with Gal. 4:19. A subsequent chapter shall draw on this idea. It, too, is rooted in the life of God *in Christ*: the goal is that all Christians become "like Him" (1 John 3:2), conformed to His image (Rom. 8:29). Here Timothy is Paul's *faithful* child (as an obedient imitator of Paul); the Corinthians are being exhorted to similar obedience. The rule should be: "Like father, like son."

7. This word is παιδαγωγός, a household slave given charge of a child's safety

and discipline; it is a far cry from a "father." "Admonishing" ($\nu o \upsilon \theta \epsilon \tau \hat{\omega} \nu$) here is especially appropriate as the work of a father, cf. Eph. 6:4 and Josephus, *Jewish War*, I, 481, where Herod threatens his sons as king and admonishes them as father. (See also H. Conzelmann, *1 Corinthians*, trans. J. W. Leitch, Hermeneia (Philadelphia: Fortress, 1975), z. St. 1 Cor. 4:14-15.

8. But mainly through his preaching; cf. 1 Cor. 1:14–17.

9. Care: Phil. 1:8; responsibility: 2 Cor. 11:28; obedience: 2 Cor. 13:10; 2 Thess. 3:14; Philemon 8; frustration: Gal. 4:20; shame/pride: 2 Cor. 3:2–3; cf. Rom. 15:16–17, where the Gentile converts being presented to God are for Paul a $\kappa\alpha\acute{\upsilon}\chi\eta\sigma\iota\varsigma$, a basis for appropriate pride and joy.

10. Where this encounter took place is debated; Rome is probable. It is doubtful that they met by chance.

11. Chapter 5 shall return to this scene, to emphasize a different point.

12. Not "I ask you for," as proposed by J. Knox on pp. 25–26 of the third edition (1935) of his *Philemon among the Letters of Paul,* cited and refuted by Donald Guthrie, *New Testament Introduction*, 3d ed. (Downers Grove: InterVarsity, 1970), pp. 635–36.

13. It may be instructive to contrast the tone here with that in Rom. 1:11–12, expressing hope of reciprocal exchange. Romans is an epistle written to Christians *not* in one of Paul's congregations, cf. Rom. 15:14–16, and the principle expressed in 15:20.

14. Thus Babylonian Talmud, San. 19b: "When a man teaches the son of another the Torah, the Scripture treats him as if he had begotten him." Cited in F. Büchsel, *et al.,* "gennaō, k.t.l.," TDNT I, 665–66. Compare also Philo, *De Legatione ad Gaium,* VIII, 58, in a remark Gaius alleged that his teacher, Macro, had made. Of course, it is a difficult matter to determine the extent to which any reference in the Talmud, which was written much later than the New Testament, can be used as evidence of linguistic usage in Paul's day; but Philo is a contemporary of Paul.

15. Martin Dibelius gives references in *An die Kolosser, Epheser an Philemon.* 3d ed. Rev. D. H. Greeven, Handbuch zum Neuen Testament, vol. 12 (Tübingen: J. C. B. Mohr [Paul Siebeck], 1953), z. St. Philemon 10.

16. Ralph Martin, *Colossians and Philemon,* New Century Bible (London: Oliphants, 1974), z. St. Philemon 10; Eduard Lohse, *Colossians and Philemon,* trans. W. Poehlmann and R. J. Karris, *Hermeneia* (Philadelphia: Fortress, 1971), p. 200.

17. See G. B. Caird, *The Language and Imagery of the Bible* (Philadelphia: Westminster, 1980), p. 152.

18. This can also be asserted of the Gnostic sources and perhaps also of the rabbis, namely, that they believed this same way, but they saw the medium of spiritual birth differently. All of this does not necessarily prove that Paul was a Platonist, but only a believer (in the Biblical tradition) that *God* is the source and goal of all. The modern analyst of human language, of course, will operate scientifically, *a la* Aristotle, from the immediate and the specific to the abstract and the general. But Caird (p. 16, n. 10) reproduces the observation of Owen Barfield (*Poetic Diction,* pp. 70ff.) that (in Caird's words) "although logically the literal precedes the metaphorical, if we look at the actual history of language, the further back we go the more figurative it becomes."

19. Ernst Lohmeyer, *Die Briefe an die Philipper, an die Kolosser und an Philemon,* 13th ed., KEK IX (Göttingen: Vandenhoeck & Ruprecht, 1964), p. 186; Conzelmann, p. 91. Lohmeyer notes that Paul here, as characteristically elsewhere ("body," "tree"), sets side by side an organic process and a religious matter.

20. It could be argued that this is such a "window onto the mysterious" (rather than "manner of speaking") only to believers in the Christian Gospel. Believers in Torah or Mithra might express their understanding of "father" in the same way. Therefore, what makes Paul special and all of this "real" for a Christian person, spiritually, is the perspective that a person's own faith gives to his reading of St. Paul.

21. This latter rendering is given, with reference to this verse, in BAGD, s. v. ὠδίνω. It is interesting to note some similar expressions in the *Confessions* of St. Augustine. In Book I, 11 (17) Augustine refers to his conversion in which also his mother had been suffering the labor pains "of his eternal salvation."

22. Despite the fact that the external evidence of the manuscript tradition favors the reading νήπιοι, "babes," this translation accepts ἤπιοι, "gentle." ἤπιοι, the uncommon word, is the more difficult reading but still renders good sense. Some argue that νήπιοι, though the more difficult reading because of the shift in metaphor involved (from "babes" to "nurses"), is still a reasonable reading because Paul "characteristically" makes such "violent" shifts. This is the rationale of the majority of the committee which worked on the text of the third edition of the United Bible Societies' *Greek New Testament* (with which the text of the 26th ed. of *Novum Testamentum Graece,* ed. K. Aland, *et al.* agrees). On pp. 629–30 of Bruce Metzger's *A Textual Commentary on the Greek New Testament* (London and New York: United Bible Societies, 1971) that majority committee opinion is supported by reference to Gal. 4:19. But there is no such "violent shift" of metaphor in that passage. Metzger himself, along with Alan Wikgren, declared his preference for ἤπιοι in a bracketed "minority opinion" note inserted on p. 630. The 25th edition of Nestle-Aland's *Novum Testamentum Graece* also read ἤπιοι, and it is also preferred by Ernest Best, *A Commentary on the First and Second Epistles to the Thessalonians,* Black's New Testament Commentaries (London: Black, 1972). An excellent article providing a view of the context of the passage is A. J. Malherbe, "Gentle as a Nurse," *Novum Testamentum,*, XII (1970), 203–17; Malherbe also prefers ἤπιοι, "gentle." The point in this section is not directly dependent on proving that the variant ἤπιοι should be read; the "mothering" language is in the word "nurses."

23. BAGD, s.v.

24. "Wet-nurse" language also is not unique to Paul. According to Malherbe, the Cynics compared a good philosopher to a gentle nurse, a combination most apt for the context of 1 Thessalonians. According to Otto Betz in "Die Geburt der Gemeinde durch den Lehrer," *New Testament Studies,* III (1957), 314–26, the relationship of the community to God through the Teacher of Righteousness is expressed in the Qumran psalms under the imagery of a nursing-father. See esp. pp. 320–22 and lQH 7:20–22; lQH 9:29–32. J. E. Frame, *A Critical and Exegetical Commentary on the Epistles of St. Paul to the Thessalonians,* ICC, vol. 38 (New York: Scribners, 1912), suggests that Paul had in mind the figure of the nursing father mentioned by Moses in Num. 11:12.

25. It is certainly to be preferred over "preacher" or "reverend."

26. Large Catechism, Fourth Commandment, 158–60. William Hulme also reflected

on the appropriateness of this in *Your Pastor's Problems* (Minneapolis: Augsburg, 1966), pp. 134–35.

27. There is a fine but important line of distinction between a pastor's accepting courtesies extended to him for the sake of his office and his active seeking of "clergy discounts" and other such (often unofficial) perquisites.

28. See Heb. 12:14–15; 13:17; Deut. 29:17. As a corollary, the ecclesiastical leadership must be responsible to consider termination of the relationship when individuals who have been entrusted with the authority and responsibility of people's spiritual lives become neglectful or abusive. Child neglect and child abuse are crimes; society steps in to put a stop to them. Congregation neglect and saint-abuse need to be swiftly and effectively addressed and dealt with by those responsible for overseeing and supervising the conduct of the ministry.

29. This whole chapter might serve also as an argument in favor of a married rather than a celibate clergy. (Physical) parenthood is an appropriate part of a pastor's education: a "hands on" "object lesson" of an important aspect of his calling and responsibility.

CHAPTER 3

1. See C. K. Barrett, *From First Adam to Last* (New York: Scribners. 1962), esp. pp. 1–21, 68–91.

2. See chaps. 8–10, esp. 9:8–15.

3. Matt. 10:24–25a, KJV. The parallel in Luke 6:40b may hint even more strongly that the *apostles* especially are similar to their Lord in being martyred as targets of murderous hatred: "And each one, when *fully trained* shall be as his master."

4. "To be baptized" in this context has the special connotation of suffering death in judgment.

5. He is *the* apostle, Heb. 3:1.

6. Note that therefore Rom. 11:26 can scarcely mean that all of ethnic Israel will at some future time be saved; if that were what Paul had understood, he would have had no reason to offer to give up his share of heaven for their sakes in 9:1–5. Rather "all Israel" in 11:26 must mean all those in Christ: believing Jews and Gentiles, saved by incorporation (ingrafting) into the true Israel, Jesus.

7. The form of the statement of the condition establishes it as *impossible*. It is a "contrary to fact" condition: "*were* it possible (granting that, in fact, it is *not* possible) .... "

8. Here Paul is not unlike the Good Samaritan, see Luke 10:35.

9. Hypotheses which break 2 Corinthians apart and suggest that chaps. 10–13 were written earlier are unnecessary; see Martin Franzmann, *The Word of the Lord Grows* (St. Louis: Concordia, 1961), pp. 107–08; and Donald Guthrie, *New Testament Introduction*, 3d ed. (Downers Grove: InterVarsity, 1970), pp. 430–37.

10. Thus the RSV, taking ὑπερλίαν ironically, and not as referring to the genuinely acknowledged "preeminent" Jerusalem apostles.

11. Dieter Georgi, *Die Gegner des Paulus im 2. Korintherbrief,* Wissenschaftliche Monoqraphien zum Alten und Neuen Testament, vol. XI (Neukirchen-Vluyn: Neukirchener, 1964), and Walter Schmithals, *Gnosticism in Corinth,* trans. John

E. Steely (Nashville: Abingdon, 1971) have argued that these false apostles represented a syncretistic Gnosticizing Judaism (probably of a type that would have been at home in Asia Minor). They consider Colossians to have been addressed to such a heresy, and Schmithals also felt that the opponents in Galatia and those referred to in the opening verses of Phil. 3 were of the same ilk. According to this view, there is no need to link these opponents of Paul to any wing of the Jerusalem church, and it is likely that their practical and doctrinal views were not too different from the aberrations reflected in 1 Corinthians. But Derk William Oostendorp, *Another Jesus* (Kampen: J. H. Kok, 1967) supported the thesis that the opponents of Paul in 2 Corinthians were Judaizing apostles who came to correct the Gospel preached by Paul by defending the superiority of Israel over the Gentiles in the new age and in the new life in Jesus Christ. At the heart of the problem is Israel, its law, and the restoration to Israel of the promised kingdom. Paul's opponents are supposedly accusing him of not having fully entered into the new age: he preaches the Gospel to Gentiles in a way that humiliates Israel. According to this view it is not necessary to see these false apostles as the same ones who were responsible for the doctrinal aberrations and the enthusiastic abuse of freedom reflected in 1 Corinthians. They really are "newcomers" on the scene.

12. *Another Jesus*, pp. 75–79.

13. ὥστε ὁ θάνατος ἐν ἡμῖν ἐνεργεῖται, ἡ δὲ ζωὴ ἐν ὑμῖν. The plural "us" is simply an "editorial" we. ἐνεργεῖται signals a supernatural power at work in the apostle as he performs his assigned role in the divine plan (economy) of salvation, cf. Gal. 2:8.

14. *Paulus, Der Bote Jesu* (Stuttgart: Calwer, 1934), p. 534.

15. Franzmann provides an eloquent characterization of Colossians' teaching of the supremacy of Christ and the all-sufficiency of His atoning sacrifice (see pp. 124–26).

16. A helpful analysis is given by Ernst Lohmeyer, *Die Briefe an die Philipper, an die Kolosser und an Philemon,* 13th ed., KEK IX (Göttingen: Vandenhoeck & Ruprecht, 1964), "Kolosser," p. 15; he labels 1:13–29 "The Gospel" and divides it into (1) "Christ" (13–20); (2) "Congregation" (21–23); and (3) "apostle" (24–29).

17. Although v. 24 is the main interest, the whole context (vv. 24–29) is translated here, with help from Lohmeyer's analysis, p. 75. Defense of the chosen translation is provided in the footnotes; further extended observations follow in the text.

18. The relative pronoun, ὅς, appears in the Western text tradition; Lohmeyer gives extensive argumentation in support of this reading (p. 75, n. 1). Especially strong is the frequent use of the relative as a connective throughout this section (1:13, 15; 2:10, 11) and in five of the six verses from 24–29. The movement in time from ἐγενόμην, "I became" (v. 23) to νῦν χαίρω, "now I rejoice" (v. 24) also suggests a closer connection of these two verses than is usually portrayed in translations or, for that matter, in the layout of the Nestle-Aland Greek text.

19. The definite article points to "sufferings—the ones of which you know I speak," cf. BDF, sec. 252. The possessive adjective may at times be an appropriate translation.

20. ὑπέρ literally means "over," "above," but according to BAGD it is never used

in a literal, local sense in the New Testament and associated literature. With the genitive it has the meaning "for," "in behalf of," and "for the sake of," to express a request for, concern about, being on someone's side, dying for, sacrifice for, in atonement for, in the stead of, the reason because of or for the sake of, in the interest of. BDF, sec. 231 discusses the tendency to interchange ὑπέρ with περί.

21. The ἀντ(ι) in this rare compound suggests that the focus *is* on suffering from Paul's side but *corresponding to* the suffering of the Christ.

22. It is not that Christ's sufferings are lacking in value, but there is a sense in which there is a quantity of His afflictions yet to take place. If a month is half gone, 15 days are the ὑστέρημα of it. When they have passed, the month will have its πλήρωμα, that which fills it up and makes it complete. The opposite of ὑστέρημα can be πλήρωμα, "full measure"; it does not have to be περίσσευμα "over-abundance." In 1 Cor. 16:17, the *presence* of Stephanus, Fortunatus, and Achaicus helps fill up (ἀνεπλήρωσαν) the absence (ὑστέρημα) of the Corinthians.

23. That is: "the church's"; the relative is feminine.

24. Paul is the servant, δοῦλος, of Jesus in Rom. 1:1; here he is the minister, διάκονος, of the Gospel (v. 23) and of the church.

25. The οἰκονομία of God is His plan of salvation (Eph. 1:10; 3:9), often with respect to specific arrangements, offices, and roles (1 Cor. 9:17; Eph. 3:2). Luke 16:2–4 speaks of a steward in his office, and (according to BAGD) the Martyrdom of Polycarp 2:2 calls the arrangement of the parts of the body beneath the skin an οἰκονομία.

26. In this, the only subsection that does not begin with a relative pronoun, the "mystery" is in apposition to the "Word of God," which it is Paul's office to fulfill with respect to the Colossians; it means the preaching of the Gospel of the one new man in Christ Jesus to Jews and Gentiles in Gentiles' lands (see Eph. 3:1–10 and Col. 1:27).

27. Read the δέ as bringing emphasis to the "now." "Mystery" is the subject of the finite verb and is in apposition to "Word of God"; hence, there is no need for a dash to indicate an anacoluthon.

28. Read, with p[46], Vaticanus, Alexandrinus and others, ὅ instead of ὅς; the antecedent is "this mystery" in the preceding line. This line names the mystery: Christ in you (Gentiles); and its wealth: the hope of glory.

29. It is better to understand this ὅν as a neuter, with "mystery" as the antecedent. This is consistent, then, with v. 27. To read this relative as referring to Christ would also cause a certain unevenness of thought as one arrives at the end of the verse. It is better to say that Paul preaches this "mystery of the Gospel" to all in order to present every man perfect in Christ than to say that he preaches "Christ" to all in order to present every man "perfect in Christ."

30. This is cultic language and reflects Paul's vision of his missionary work as priestly service (cf. Rom. 15:16; also Rom. 12:1–2). At the end-time he will offer to God his converts, taught, perfect, without blemish. They are the "fruits" of his "labor" (v. 29) for God. Cf. also Phil. 2:14–18.

31. Casting v. 29 as three lines instead of two is a departure from Lohmeyer's scheme. ἐνέργεια is the powerful work of supernatural presences *in* something of this world (Eph. 1:19; Col. 2:12; and also 2 Thess. 2:9, Satan, and 2:11,

113

deception, BAGD). Here it refers to the power of the grace of God at work specifically in Paul's office as an apostle; the verse clearly is related to Gal. 2:8; cf. Eph. 3:20.

32. See, for example, Eduard Lohse, *Colossians and Philemon,* trans. W. R. Poehlmann and R. J. Karris (Philadelphia: Fortress, 1971), p. 73.

33. Albeit perhaps not in every detail within the larger section.

34. With the exception (see n. 31) that the last subsection is cast as a three-line piece instead of two lines.

35. J. B. Lightfoot, *Saint Paul's Epistles to the Colossians and to Philemon* (Grand Rapids: Zondervan, 1959; reprint of 1879 ed.), p. 164. The contrast is to an earlier time when Paul did not yet see this so fully.

36. The movement from the past tense ("I became," v. 23) to the present tense ("I rejoice," v. 24) called for the "now." See Lohmeyer, p. 75, n. 1.

37. Lohse, p. 69, n. 10, citing Karl Staab.

38. Lohmeyer, p. 74.

39. Ibid., p. 76.

40. Ibid.

41. Compare Rev. 8:6–9:11 to Ex. 7–10.

42. See Matt. 24:8–9, 21–22 and parallels. Similarly, the Syriac Apoc. of Baruch (2 Baruch) 25:1–3 says: "And he answered and said to me: 'You also will be preserved until that time, namely until that sign which the Most High will bring about before the inhabitants of the earth at the end of days. This will be the sign: when horror seizes the inhabitants of the earth, and they fall into many tribulations and further, they fall into great torments.'" (Trans. from CW I, 629; cf. 4 Esdras 9:1–4.)

43. Implicit in Jesus' words to Saul on the road to Damascus, Acts 9:4, and explicit in 1 Peter 4:13.

44. Lohse names Adolf Deissmann and others, p. 69, n. 11.

45. See Lightfoot, pp. 164–66, even though he does not make much progress beyond this view. It is criticized also by Lohmeyer, pp. 77–78, who points out that according to this interpretation the idea of the ὑστέρημα is meaningless.

46. Lightfoot, p. 166, commenting on ἀνταναπληρῶ.

47. Ibid., pp. 166–67, described this benefit with his widely-noted distinction between satisfactory sufferings and edificatory sufferings. Only Christ's sufferings are satisfaction for sin; these sufferings of which Paul speaks here are the afflictions of every saint and martyr. They supplement the afflictions of Christ by being edificatory. The *benefit* is that the church is built up by repeated acts of self-denial in successive individuals and successive generations. But this fails to account for the phrase that calls them the "afflictions of the *Christ.*"

48. *Colossians,* pp. 70–72.

49. Cf. Acts 14:22, where Paul exhorted that "through many tribulations (θλίψεων) we must enter the kingdom of God."

50. ὑπὲρ τῆς ὑμῶν παρακλήσεως.

51. Lohse, pp. 70–71, does note that Paul, in his office as an apostle, is to be differentiated from the community. But he specifically rejects the view elaborated next ("apostolic ministry") and maintains that the *benefit* is in the con-

tribution made to the filling up of the fixed amount of sufferings in the "messianic woes."

52. *Der Brief an die Kolosser,* Evangelisch-Katholischer Kommentar zum Neuen Testament (Zürich: Henziger, 1976), pp. 82–86. Schweizer's presentation is complicated unnecessarily by his distinction between the views of Paul and those represented in Colossians, which he takes to be post-Pauline. Paul himself, Schweizer says, connects his sufferings to his apostolic service (2 Cor. 4:10) and makes it clear in what sense his suffering is for the benefit of the church (2 Cor. 1:3–11): (1) in that he learns comfort and thereby learns to comfort; (2) in that he learns what faith in the God who resurrects from the dead really means; and (3) in that he enters a fellowship of intercession and thanksgiving with his congregation. His suffering also is of benefit in that it lets his message be ratified as credible and be unfolded clearly in all its power. But what is asserted in Colossians, according to Schweizer, goes beyond what Paul would say; the "for you" formulation here is "foreign to Paul."

53. In combination with the "messianic woes" line of interpretation, *Kolosser,* p. 78.

54. *Was an den Leiden Christi noch Mangelt,* Bonner Biblische Beiträge, vol. 12 (Bonn: Hanstein, 1956), esp. pp. 189–95. Kremer's position is reviewed by Ernst Käsemann in *Theologische Literaturzeitung* 82 (1957), 694–95. Erhardt Güttgemanns' monograph, *Der leidende Apostel und sein Herr,* Forschungen zur Religion und Literatur des Alten und Neuen Testaments, no. 90 (Göttingen: Vandenhoeck & Ruprecht, 1966), also makes an important contribution towards understanding the passage under this line of interpretation.

55. Schweizer, p. 91. Schweizer seems to hear Paul himself describing a special intensity with which an apostle, in the mystical union, shares in the messianic woes (pp. 82–85); thus he tries to fuse all three of the lines of interpretation here described. But he acknowledges that this passage in Colossians (post-Pauline, in his view) raises the problem of the relationship of the *saving event* to the *proclamation* of the saving event (pp. 89–90). This hints at the question of the relationship of the *apostolic ministry* to the ministry of the Savior Himself. This, in turn, impinges upon the concerns of the "new hermeneutic" and also upon the debate as to whether or not ordination is a sacrament. Charles E. Winquist explores the impact of the "new hermeneutic" ("word as event instead of word as content") on the understanding of the ministry in *Practical Hermeneutics* (Chico: Scholars Press, 1980).

56. Schweizer, p. 86. He allows that there may be in this Colossians passage an overtone of the thought that the apostle's life is likened unto *(angeglichen)* that of Jesus.

57. Lohmeyer, p. 79; author's translation.

58. *Leidende Apostel,* pp. 116–17, author's translation. The German reads: "Paulus ist mit seinem σῶμα 'gleichsam selber Erscheinungsweise des Christus incarnatus nach dessen Himmelfahrt.'" The reference is to Käsemann in *Zeitschrift für die Neutestamentliche Theologie* 41 (1942), 56.

59. See Güttgemanns, p. 118 and n. 136 on the "epiphany-character" of the apostle's sufferings.

60. That the ministry may be referred to as a sacrament is supported by Art. XIII of the Apology of the Augsburg Confession, especially when read in conjunction

with the contents and position of Art. V of the Augsburg Confession itself; see esp. Ap XIII, 7–13.

61. Francis Pieper points out the need for a true theologian to be ready to *suffer.* See *Christian Dogmatics* (St. Louis: Concordia, 1950), I:51.

62. An attempt at a graphic schematization might look like this:

sacrifices		sufferings
——————————————→ CHRIST ←——————————————		
lives of prophets		lives of apostles (and those in the ministry)
TYPOLOGY		IMITATION

63. Today designated *by God* but *mediately,* as He works through orderly procedures within the church; but *not* designated solely *by* the church as a democratic assembly which is *delegating its* powers and responsibilities.

64. Recent titles include Charles Rassieur, *Stress Management for Ministers* (Philadelphia: Westminster, 1982), and John A. Sanford, *Ministry Burnout* (New York: Paulist, 1982); see also Winton H. Beaven, "Ministerial burnout—cause and prevention," *Ministry* 59 (1986): 4–7, 20.

Chapter 4

1. The first line of a hymn by Martin Luther, trans. Catherine Winkworth, No. 261 in *The Lutheran Hymnal* (St. Louis: Concordia, 1941).

2. Is. 7:9b, author's trans.; the Hebrew is: *im lo ta'amīnū kī lo tē'āmēnū.*

3. Hab. 2:4; Rom. 1:17; Gal. 3:11; Heb. 10:38.

4. Author's trans. of Hab. 2:4b; the Hebrew is: *wᵉtsaddīq be'emūnāthō yihyeh.*

5. This is the RSV translation, which we have retained in keeping with the title of our chapter; literally, it says: "I am zealous over you with zeal of God."

6. Compare the servant's characterization of the king in the parable of the minas, Luke 19:21: "for I was afraid of you, because you are a severe man; you take up what you did not lay down, and reap what you did not sow" (RSV).

7. See Luke 15:6–7, 9–10, 32.

8. There is "good" jealousy and "bad," as well as zeal that is "noble" and zeal that is not. It depends upon its motives, object, and context. Jealousy is a vice as used in Rom. 13:13; 1 Cor. 3:3; Gal. 5:20. It is not inherently bad in Rom. 10:2 and Phil. 3:6, but only misdirected. On the other hand, it is a good thing in 2 Cor. 7:7, 11; 9:2; and (in the verb form) in 1 Cor. 12:31; 14:1, 39.

9. This goes beyond C. K. Barrett, *A Commentary on the Second Epistle to the Corinthians,* Black's New Testament Commentaries (London: Black, 1973), p. 272, who says it is the Corinthians' own responsibility.

10. See 2 Cor. 1:14: the Corinthians are to be Paul's καύχημα. See Barrett's instructive comments, pp. 73–74.

11. See also Gal. 2:2; 3:4; 2 Cor. 6:1; 1 Thess. 3:5.

12. This is one possible meaning for ζηλόω, BAGD, s.v.

13. "Are solicitous of you" can also be used consistently to render this verb throughout this passage.

14. It is a selfish and human jealousy, not "of God."

15. From what? From the fellowship of their circle of Jewish Christian, more highly privileged, "first-class citizens" of the kingdom of Israel?

16. This translation reads the infinitive, rejecting the few (but strong) witnesses for the imperative. Also to be preferred is the reading without τό; on the propriety of the infinitive as subject without the definite article when there is no anaphoric reference, see BDF, sec. 399. English requires this translation of the passive or else the use of a different verb, "be courted," or "be loved jealously."

17. For a review of the twisted history of the attempts to describe the agitators in Galatia, see George Howard, *Paul: Crisis in Galatia,* Societas Novi Testamenti Studiorum Monograph, 35 (Cambridge: Cambridge University Press, 1979).

18. See Robert Jewett, "The Agitators and the Galatian Congregation," *New Testament Studies,* 17 (1970–71), 198–212.

19. Not the "party" described by Josephus as one of the factions in Jerusalem at the end of the Jewish War, but those in the tradition of Phineas, Mattathias, Judas the Galilean and his sons (who were crucified under Tiberius Alexander, A.D. 46–48, according to Josephus, *Antiquities* XX, 102).

20. It is feasible that "that you might be zealous for them" includes also the deference and financial support which Jewish Christians, as "first-class citizens" of the kingdom, were demanding from Gentile Christians, as Oostendorp describes the situation in Corinth, *Another Jesus* (Kampen: J. H. Kok, 1967), pp. 75–79.

21. It is most logical to envision the towns of "South Galatia," but precisely where does not matter for the point being made here.

22. Gal. 4:16. See H. D. Betz, *Galatians, Hermeneia* (Philadelphia: Fortress, 1979), p. 228, n. 99, and Cicero, *De Amicitia,* 89–104.

23. This is well expounded in Martin Luther's 1535 commentary, and clearly reiterated by G. Ebeling, *The Truth of the Gospel,* trans. D. Green (Philadelphia: Fortress, 1985).

24. What is Paul? A servant through whom you believed (1 Cor. 3:5). Paul (and all things) are yours, and you are Christ's, and Christ is God's (1 Cor. 3:21–23).

25. See the references to those who "appear" to be important, Gal. 2:2, 6, 9.

26. In Gal. 1:8 Paul makes it clear that it is not the identity, origin, or status of the messenger that certifies the message, but rather that the message is the way to test the legitimacy of the messenger. See J. H. Schütz, *Paul and the Anatomy of Apostolic Authority,* Societas Novi Testamenti Studiorum Monograph, 26 (Cambridge: Cambridge University Press, 1975).

27. In *Enemies of the Roman Order* (Cambridge: Harvard University Press, 1966), Ramsay Macmullen documents that political unrest in A.D. 50–100 centered around such literary men and philosophers. The thought that a great change is imminent, with the appearance (παρουσία) of a new lord (κύριος) whom we shall encounter in a formal meeting (ἀπάντησις) but whose coming someone or something is presently restraining—all of this might not have seemed such strange talk to the Thessalonians. In *The Thessalonian Correspondence*

(Philadelphia: Fortress, 1986), Robert Jewett described not only the political, but also the sociological and religious contexts of Paul's preaching in Thessalonica. A. J. Malherbe also showed, especially, the connections of 1 Thess. 2 to language used by Cynic-Stoic teachers to uphold the integrity of their activities.

28. Ζηλώσαντες, "being zealous," Acts 17:5.

29. ὅτι νῦν ζῶμεν ἐὰν ὑμεῖς στήκετε ἐν κυρίῳ.

30. BDF, sec. 73.

31. BAGD, s.v.: a relationship to the hiphil and niphal of 'mn is possible, yielding the nuance: "If you continue to let yourself be caused to stand in the Lord."

32. BDF, sec. 372 (1a).

33. Ernest Best, *A Commentary on the First and Second Epistles to the Thessalonians,* Black's New Testament Commentaries (London: Black, 1972), p. 142.

34. D. E. H. Whiteley, *Thessalonians,* The New Clarendon Bible (Oxford: Oxford University Press, 1969), p. 54.

35. Recall the significance of the words that Paul heard Jesus say on the road to Damascus. Saul was on his way to extradite followers of the "Way" to Jerusalem when Jesus appeared to him and said: "Saul, Saul, why are you persecuting *me?*" He did not say "my followers," but "*me.*" The believers *are* the body of Christ in the world. They are, "though many, . . . one body in Christ and individually members one of another" (Rom. 12:5).

36. I. Howard Marshall comments aptly in *1 and 2 Thessalonians,* New Century Bible (Grand Rapids: Eerdmans, 1983), p. 96: [Paul] felt that his life was so bound up with that of his converts that when they showed signs of spiritual weakness he himself felt involved and weakened . . . . But at the same time the presence of the Spirit in Paul meant that a new life was being communicated to him. . . . And among the means by which this spiritual life was nurtured there was the growth in life and spiritual strength of Paul's converts.

37. BDF, sec. 452(2): γάρ gives the reason for a tacit answer of "yes"; see 1 Cor. 9:10.

38. A "crown of boasting"; the crown (στέφανος, cf. 1 Cor. 9:25) is the symbol of victory conferred by another upon a champion or conqueror. The "boasting" can only be that appropriate pride based on God's work through Paul's apostolic ministry. See Best, p. 128; and F. F. Bruce, *1 and 2 Thessalonians,* Word Biblical Commentary, 45 (Waco: Word, 1982), p. 58, who makes the point that this cannot and does not contradict Gal. 6:14.

39. Perhaps here in the sense of "source of good repute," or "a credit to me" (cf. 2 Cor. 8:23 and Bruce, p. 57).

40. Best, p. 129.

41. Although it is not only apostles who have "work, toil" to do as a result of having received grace: see 1 Tim. 5:17 (elders); 1 Cor. 16:16; 1 Thess. 5:12; and also 2 Cor. 6:1, where Paul appeals to the Corinthians themselves not to receive the grace of God in vain.

42. The word "toil," inept as it may be at times, here stands for κόπος and its cognates; it differs from ἔργα, "deeds" or "works," which Paul regularly uses in a theologically pejorative sense, as in the phrase "works of law."

43. Col. 1:28–9: "Him we proclaim, warning every man and teaching every man

in all wisdom, that we may present every man mature in Christ. For this I toil, striving with all the energy which He mightily inspires within me" (RSV); cf. 1 Tim. 4:10.

44. 1 Cor. 15:10–11: "But by the gracious and powerful gift of God I am what I am [namely, an apostle], and His gift did not come for naught. On the contrary, I toiled harder than they, though it was not I, but the gracious power of God which is with me. Whether then it was I or they, so we preach and so you believed."

45. 1 Cor. 3:8 declares the equality of "he who plants" and "he who waters" and states that each shall receive his reward according to his toil. In Gal. 2:7–9 the apostles agree on their designated spheres of work. See also 1 Cor. 15:10 (n. 44 above) and 2 Cor. 11:23.

46. In 2 Cor. 10:13–15 Paul establishes that his boasting has to do with the Corinthians, because he was the first to bring the Gospel to them, "For we do not boast beyond limit, in other men's labors; but our hope is that as your faith increases, our field among you may be greatly enlarged, so that we may preach the gospel in lands beyond you, without boasting of work already done in another's field" (vv. 15–16, RSV). See also Rom. 15:18–21; 2 Tim. 2:6; and 1 Thess. 2:20, above.

47. In Rom. 1:13 Paul expresses the desire to reap some harvest among the Romans as also among the rest of the Gentiles' lands, and in Col. 1:16 he speaks of the Gospel bearing fruit in faith throughout the whole world. In 1 Cor. 15:14, the focus is on the truth of the actual resurrection of Jesus, without which both Paul's toil (preaching) and its fruit (their faith) would be for naught.

48. 2 Cor. 11:2; Col. 1:28–9; and Phil. 2:14–16: "Do all things without grumbling or questioning, that you may be blameless and innocent, children of God without blemish in the midst of a crooked and perverse generation, among whom you shine as lights in the world, holding fast the word of life, so that in the day of Christ I may be proud that I did not run or labor in vain" (RSV).

49. Or "running," Gal. 2:2; Phil. 2:16.

50. Gal. 4:11; 1 Thess. 3:5.

51. He might have then been considered to be like the fearful steward in the parable of the pounds, Luke 19:11–27.

52. In contrast to the opponents in Corinth, who strive for a pride founded on the wrong basis, 2 Cor. 5:12.

53. Ernst Lohmeyer, *Die Briefe an die Philipper, an die Kolosser und an Philemon,* 13th ed., KEK IX (Göttingen: Vandenhoeck & Ruprecht, 1964), *Philipper,* pp. 110–11, author's trans.

54. Charts of wondrous administrative models and snappy sayings about "making" congregations "forces" instead of "fields" do not help.

CHAPTER 5

1. Rom. 8:20–22. Futility is failure to have actual results conform to God's intended results.

2. This must be said very clearly, in the face of the current tendency to emphasize

this-worldly aspects of *shalom,* as, for example, W. Foerster and G. von Rad do in TDNT II, 400–20.

3. Jer. 31:31–34. John Donne prayed:

> ... oh! of Thine only worthy blood,
> And my tears, make a heavenly Lethean flood,
> And drown in it my sins' black memory;
> That Thou remember them, some claim as debt,
> I think it mercy, if Thou wilt forget. (Holy Sonnets, IX)

as found in: John Donne, *Selected Poetry,* ed. Marius Bewley, *The Signet Classic Poetry Series* (New York: New American Library, 1966), p. 269.

4. A recent monograph by Ralph Martin, *Reconciliation: A Study of Paul's Theology,* New Foundations Theological Library (Atlanta: John Knox, 1981), suggests that "reconciliation" is "the keyword of Paul's Gospel so far as its working out in Christ is concerned" (p. 3).

5. Rom. 5:1, reading the indicative form, ἔχομεν. Even if the subjunctive form is taken to be the correct textual reading, a declaratory indicative must lie beneath the Pauline exhortation. It might then be paraphrased: "Having been justified, therefore, by faith, let us be encouraged to enjoy and to live in the peace with God [*given*] through our Lord Jesus Christ."

6. See also τὰ πάντα, "all things," Col. 1:20.

7. This could become a point of departure for a discussion of the proper involvement of the church in ecology—ecology in its finest sense: the proper interrelationship of all created things under God and with man as His steward. Ministers of the Gospel and the people of God whose life they nurture should, indeed, be in the forefront as examples of true stewardship and illustrations of the consequences of the reconciliation and restoration of peace and wholeness that they preach in Christ. Everything said here about "filling the gap" between people may be extended and applied to the expression of concern for the entire creation. But the focus in this chapter shall be on the consequences in person-to-person relationships.

8. Rom. 15:7, as rendered by the RSV. This relatively weak English word, however, hardly expresses the full significance of *receiving* someone into *fellowship* that is carried in the Greek word, προσλαμβάνεσθε.

9. Rev. Oswald Waech applied this phrase from Philemon to the whole paradigm of ministry described in this section in a sermon he preached at Christ the King Lutheran Church, Walnut, CA, while he was serving the Southern California District of The Lutheran Church—Missouri Synod.

10. Previous chapters have already alluded to several verses of Philemon. This section takes up the whole historical situation in detail, as a paradigm of peacemaking ministry. The epistle raises several weighty theological points of discussion. It should not be considered insignificant because it is short, and it should not be passed over either in preaching or in Bible classes.

11. See Donald Guthrie, *New Testament Introduction,* 3d ed. (Downers Grove: InterVarsity, 1970) pp. 472–78, 635; and Eduard Lohse, *Colossians and Philemon,* trans. W. R. Poehlmann and R. J. Karris, *Hermeneia* (Philadelphia: Fortress, 1971), pp. 187–88, where he espouses the hypothesis of an Ephesian origin of the epistle.

12. "Paul and Onesimus," *Harvard Theological Review* 22 (1929), 181–83. The applicability of this asylum practice to the situation encountered in Philemon is also accepted by Lohse, p. 187, and by Ernst Lohmeyer, *Die Briefe and die Philipper, an die Kolosser und an Philemon,* 13th ed. KEK IX (Göttingen: Vandenhoeck & Ruprecht, 1964), *Philemon,* p. 172, where he provides further references to document the widespread practice of the custom.

13. ... διὰ τὴν ἀγάπην, v. 9. "For love's sake," yes, but not the love of a master for a runaway slave, but rather because of the love of God in Christ which has also been poured out into our hearts (Rom. 5:5, 8).

14. Philemon 8, 19b, RSV; "self" in 19b is σεαυτόν.

15. Philemon 12; the Greek is: ... αὐτόν, τοῦτ᾽ ἔστιν τὰ ἐμὰ σπλάγχνα. KJV renders σπλάγχνα as "bowels," RSV as "heart," NEB as "a part of myself."

16. For we all are "God's Onesimuses," as Martin Luther noted in his *Prefaces to the New Testament,* trans. C. M. Jacobs, rev. E. T. Bachmann (St. Louis: Concordia, n.d.), p. 36.

17. The preaching of the Christian Gospel did not issue into a social-reform movement for the abolition of slavery. Rather, the Gospel assumed from the very first the institution of the new age and all of its relationships, which transcend and transform the relationships of the old world. For an excellent discussion, see E. G. Sclwyn, *The First Epistle of St. Peter* (New York: Macmillan, 1969), pp. 103–05.

18. Even as our sacerdotal mediator, Jesus, is the ἔγγυος, Heb. 7:22.

19. This means more than just adapting "conflict management" techniques to the life of the institutional church, as Donald E. Bossart attempts to do in *Creative Conflict in Religious Education and Church Administration* (Birmingham: Religious Education Press, 1980).

20. "Woe to me," Paul said, "if I do not preach the Gospel" (1 Cor. 9:16; but be sure to read Chapter 8, below, also!).

CHAPTER 6

1. It is a compromise to translate this difficult word with any single English equivalent; to the usual "imitator" could be added "echo-mirror-facsimile-counterpart" to name just a few possibilities. It is not shallow or external imitation, but a matter of absorption and internalization followed by reflection and representation. Willis Peter De Boer has made a thorough study of the concept in *The Imitation of Paul* (Kampen: J. H. Kok, 1962). He notes the import of the concept in Greek aesthetics and ethics as well as in the Jewish understanding of the relationship of a rabbi and his disciples (see esp. chaps. 1 and 3). He concluded that at its root, the word "carried the thought of bringing to expression, representation, portrayal," a portrayal that extended to "the development of character" and "the formation of one's customs, way, and way of life," (p. 15).

2. His baptism and subsequent sojourn in the wilderness recapitulate the typological pattern of Israel, Mark 1:9–15.

3. In the Jewish understanding of discipleship, an imitator, cf. John 13:15–16.

4. 1 Peter 2:9; 2 Peter 1:4: θείας κοινωνοὶ φύσεως.

5. See De Boer, chaps. 1–3. The great shortcoming, of course, of the non-Biblical traditions of learning by imitation is in the underestimation of the power of sin. It does not follow that "to see" and "to know" what is right can lead to *doing* it; cf. Rom. 7:15–23.

6. Even as Jesus is never example without first being Savior, so also Paul does not really "teach ethics" so much as he describes the consequences of the presence of the liberating Spirit in the lives of new creatures in Christ.

7. Note the context of the verse, amidst the long ethical exhortation of Eph. 4:1–6:20.

8. Reading the genitive as objective gives this sense, as in BAGD, s.v. συμμιμηταί. It cannot be "join me in becoming an imitator," because the use of the genitive with compounds in συν- does not apply to this word, BDF, sec. 194(2).

9. "You" is emphatic, in contrast to the last phrase of v. 5. The sense is: " . . . you know what sort [of people] we were among you for your sake, and you your-selves, on your part . . . . "

10. The form is passive; the verb is a middle deponent, but in Koine Greek passive forms tended to be used beside the middles in the aorist. It could be and often is translated "become." See BDF, sec. 78, and an extensive report of the views of grammarians in De Boer, pp. 99–100; he notes that if it is a true passive, God is the hidden subject.

11. "Welcomed" might be chosen to bring out the positive connotations of the word; see BAGD s.v. δέχομαι and note the examples under meaning 1., even though this passage is listed under 3.b.

12. It is best to consider ἐν as the equivalent of ἐν μέσῳ.

13. This is a genitive of origin: it is a joy whose genesis is in God the Holy Spirit.

14. De Boer, pp. 97–98, 108, notes that the chain of thought, which begins with thanksgiving and moves on to Paul's preaching of the Gospel, the divine work-ing in the hearers, imitation, and finally to suffering, recurs in 2:13–14, where Paul picks up his train of thought again. Many commentators feel that the "thanksgiving" extends into 1 Thess. 3, as reported in F. F. Bruce, *1 & 2 Thessalonians,* Word Biblical Commentary 45 (Waco: Word, 1982), p. 11.

15. In other contexts the form is imperative; see below.

16. This undoubtedly refers to the hostility of the unbelieving Jews in Thessalonica.

17. So translated by the RSV.

18. See De Boer, pp. 118–19, who includes all three, but appends: "particularly of Paul himself, the leader and dominating figure."

19. This is very clear if one reads the ὅτι in v. 5 as "for."

20. See De Boer, pp. 120–21, for various views; he points out that elsewhere Paul does speak of imitating himself with no apparent need of such a *correction.*

21. I. Howard Marshall, *1 and 2 Thessalonians,* New Century Bible Commentary (Grand Rapids: Eerdmans, 1983), pp. 54–55; cf. De Boer, p. 122.

22. De Boer, p. 122, n. 102, also notes Luke 10:21 in its context as an instance of Jesus' Spirit-inspired joy in the face of hostility.

23. James E. Frame, *A Critical and Exegetical Commentary on the Epistles of St. Paul to the Thessalonians,* ICC (New York: Scribners, 1912), p. 82.

24. Cf. Phil. 2:6–11, and TDNT III, 188–90.

25. De Boer, p. 123. Thus it is clear that reception of the Word, coming to faith, is the indispensable first step; no other imitation is possible apart from this.

26. Martin Franzmann, *The Word of the Lord Grows* (St. Louis: Concordia, 1961), pp. 71–72. But De Boer, pp. 127–29, feels that this is an inference, and not an entirely justified one. He considers the disorderliness to stem from Gnostic enthusiasm (p. 133). In *The Thessalonian Correspondence* (Philadelphia: Fortress, 1986), Robert Jewett rejects both of these positions and links the problems in Thessalonica to a misappropriation of the Gospel by hearers seeking a millenarian hope similar to that of the Cabirus cult.

27. Rejected are theories of the non-Pauline authorship of 2 Thessalonians; see the discussion in Donald Guthrie, *New Testament Introduction,* 3d ed. (Downers Grove: InterVarsity, 1970), pp. 569–79.

28. The command in v. 6 to stay away from anyone who does not abide in the tradition Paul taught is grounded in the necessity of what is stated in v. 7a.

29. "How ye ought" (KJV) is too weak; it is a matter of divine necessity that the Christians be conformed to the image of the Son of God.

30. Theological (if not purely linguistic) considerations suggest that the force of this middle deponent be expanded: "that you let yourselves be made to be imitators (and imitations) of us . . . . "

31. See BAGD, s.v. ἀτακτέω, ἄτακτος, and ἀτάκτως; see also Bruce, p. 205.

32. "Eat bread" means "take food," "receive maintenance" (cf. 2 Sam. 9:7), Marshall, pp. 121–22.

33. Luke 10:7–8; cf. 1 Cor. 9:4–5, 14.

34. This articular infinitive can express purpose or result, BDF, sec. 402(2).

35. See Marshall, p. 221.

36. This is not the main point here, but it is in 1 Cor. 11:1, below.

37. 1 Cor. 4:6, NEB, which is a bold attempt, and a good one, to handle some of the linguistic difficulties in this verse. De Boer, pp. 140–43, notes and discusses various views on μετεσχημάτισα and ἃ γέγραπται.

38. See 1 Cor. 4:14–15 and Chapter 2, above.

39. That this appeal is rooted in the father-child relationship is De Boer's main thesis, pp. 145–46, 166, and Proposition I.

40. This is not an epistolary but a true aorist, cf. 1 Cor. 16:10 and the lack of any mention of Timothy in the salutation; De Boer, p. 146, n. 169, and C. K. Barrett, *A Commentary on the First Epistle to the Corinthians,* 2d ed. (London: Black, 1971), p. 116.

41. De Boer, p. 151.

42. Of course, all who follow them.

43. De Boer, pp. 150–51.

44. As De Boer says: "The imitation of Paul was to take place along the entire front of life. When he appeals to the Corinthians to be imitators of himself, basically he appeals to them to renew their efforts and recapture their original keenness and vigor in the entire matter of Christian living" (p, 154).

45. While it is not closely connected in the chain of argumentation to this verse, it is interesting to note the reference to all "the traditions . . . I have delivered" in the very next verse, 11:2.

46. Including the right to be supported, as in 2 Thess. 3:7–9.

47. De Boer, pp. 168, 213–15; the point was also made by Martin Franzmann in his essays on *Scripture and Interpretation* (Concordia Seminary Print Shop), pp. 36–49.

48. To use an old cliché; but see De Boer, p. 154, who says as much.

49. It is not necessary here to discuss the possible different meanings of each of these designations. They each describe "an office" within "the office" of the ministry.

50. 1 Cor. 16:17; Rom. 16:9, 12; Phil. 4:2–3.

51. J. A. Bengel, as quoted in Franzmann, *The Word of the Lord Grows,* p. 161.

52. As Paul wrote to Timothy in 1 Tim. 4:12: "Let no one despise your youth, but set the believers an example in speech and conduct, in love, in faith, in purity."

53. 1 Tim. 1:16; see De Boer, pp. 196–99.

54. See also Richard John Neuhaus, "The Pursuit of Holiness," ch. 11 in *Freedom for Ministry: A Critical Affirmation of the Church and Its Mission* (San Francisco: Harper & Row, 1979).

55. Paul also repudiates the idea that he himself has attained to "perfection," Phil. 3:12.

56. Just as also in the Old Testament the rules for outward cleanliness and ritual purity are applied with greater strictness and intensity to the bodies and the lives of the priests, the greater "holiness" of the servant testifies to the holiness of God, who is bridging the gap between holy God and sinful humanity through the ministry of these servants who have been set aside to draw near to Him and handle these holy things.

57. See the warning in Luke 17:2.

CHAPTER 7

1. Cf. Rom. 1:25; 2 Kings 17:15.

2. Jer. 5:31; cf. Micah 2:11; 1 Kings 22:1–28.

3. Acts 14:3; cf. Phil. 1:1; Acts 20:18–35.

4. 1 Tim. 4:6–16; 6:20–21; Titus 1:5–14.

5. This phenomenon, supposedly visible in the letters of Ignatius of Antioch, is part of what is sometimes referred to as "incipient Catholicism." For further discussion see R. P. Martin, *New Testament Foundations* (Grand Rapids: Eerdmans, 1978) II, 380–83.

6. This is presented very well by John Schütz, *Paul and the Anatomy of Apostolic Authority,* Societas Novi Testamenti Studiorum Monograph, 26 (Cambridge: Cambridge University Press, 1975).

7. See, e.g., Rom. 1:2; 3:21–4:25; 10:4–13.

8. The phrase "their true meaning," however, reveals the matter of the key to the right understanding of the Old Testament. The Spirit of the Lord lifts the veil so as to show that the Old Testament Scriptures do indeed point to Jesus Christ, 1 Cor. 3:4–18; 1 Cor. 2:9–16; cf. Rom. 10:4.

9. The Bible is *not* "the church's book" in the sense that the church, in a historical process, determined its contents. The process of the definition of the canon

is a matter of *recognizing* documents that authenticate themselves as Word of God.

10. ὑπηκούσατε δὲ ἐκ καρδίας εἰς ὃν παρεδόθητε τύπον διδαχῆς.

11. Compare Gal. 4:9: " . . . but now that you have come to know God, or rather to be known by God . . . ."

12. The Word of God is somewhat like a tiger, in this regard: let it out of its cage and it will defend itself.

13. See Schütz, pp. 116–23. It was in keeping with the same insight that Luther remarked, in his prefaces to James and Jude, that a document that upheld the Gospel was "apostolic" even if not written by an apostle, whereas a writing that tore down the Gospel was not "apostolic," even if an "apostle" wrote it, *Prefaces to the New Testament,* trans. C. M. Jacobs, rev. E. T. Bachmann (St. Louis: Concordia, n.d.), p. 45.

14. It is difficult to determine where to close the quotation begun in v. 14; see F. F. Bruce, *The Epistle to the Galatians,* The New International Greek Testament Commentary (Grand Rapids: Eerdmans, 1982), pp. 136–37. It seems wise to take vv. 15–21 as Paul's formulation of the *proposition,* a concise summary of the legal content of the case; vv. 11–14 then, are the *narratio,* a telling of the facts of the case. See Hans Dieter Betz, *Galatians, Hermeneia* (Philadelphia: Fortress, 1979), pp. 113–15.

15. The connecting particle shows that this incident is told in the context of the agreement described in Gal. 2:9.

16. Commentators to this point have failed to provide a good explanation for the use of Cephas instead of Peter in this section.

17. This means it was in person; it was also in public, as can be seen in v. 14.

18. The phrase suggests that Paul is only verbalizing the logic of the situation, in which the inconsistency of Peter's behavior with his own words is really what "condemns" him.

19. It is possible, but not certain, that these are "Judaizers," or members of a "circumcision party." James himself repudiates any connections with Judaizers who cause trouble in Acts 15:24.

20. Note the isolation of Paul on this occasion: all the Jews—and even Barnabas, his fellow missionary to the Galatians—go with Peter. But that does not deter Paul. He has his eye on the cross and he knows the truth when he sees it. He and Barnabas appear not to have been a "team" any more after this incident, cf. Bruce, pp. 131–32.

21. With this question it becomes apparent that Peter's action signaled not just a desire for "separate but equal" tables, but agreement with the opinion that Gentile Christians were (in the Jewish definition) "sinners," with whom one was not to fellowship unless they had been circumcised.

22. See this theme in the recent exposition of Galatians by Gerhard Ebeling, *The Truth of the Gospel,* trans. David Green (Philadelphia: Fortress, 1985).

23. Thus it is very Pauline that the doctrine of justification by grace for Christ's sake through faith be the touchstone of all theology, including the doctrines of church and ministry.

24. This is what Paul means when he says that it is a "small thing" to him that any man should judge him, 1 Cor. 4:3–4.

25. A provocative examination of "Manipulation and Freedom in the New Testament" in the light of the church's exercise of authority is to be found in Graham Shaw, *The Cost of Authority* (Philadelphia: Fortress, 1982). That church functionaries have abused power cannot be denied, that such abuse has been systemic since the apostolic church, as Shaw seems to argue, is not the case.

26. The legal and medical professions have recognized that they need their own codes of ethics and self-policing mechanisms. It is interesting to note that medical malpractice suits have increased as doctors have been perceived to be less and less the *servants* of those entrusted to their care and more and more the exploiters who profit from the fact of human disease. When pastors become the targets of similar litigation or even just the subject of general criticism, it could be an indication of a loss of respect due to a similar betrayal of their servant role. This means that even isolated "problem cases" must be handled expeditiously, for the sake of the entire ministerium. In any case, a congregation must not be left with the erroneous notion that they themselves "hire and fire" pastors and that they are the "bestowers" or "delegators" of the authority of the office of the ministry. The goal is always quality ministry, and the consistent application of rigorous standards must be the norm.

27. They *must* be spared the ordeal of having to turn, as a body, against the person whom they had been enjoined to obey and perhaps had even begun to adhere to as their spiritual leader.

28. There is no account from Peter concerning the incident in Antioch and no report of the effect of Paul's words on him. Subsequent history suggests that the correctness of Paul's point was eventually acknowledged.

29. This entire paragraph, vv. 1–5, is helpful. Each person is accountable (v. 5), and so each should submit his own work to the test (v. 4). But all help each other (v. 2), and no one dare think that he is something he is not (v. 3).

30. Note that part of the context of this verse is defense against human cunning and deceit (v. 14) under the graces bestowed for the ministry (v. 11). Clearly, therefore, the truth is the revealed truth of God's Word and the love is the love of God in Christ poured into our hearts through the Holy Spirit.

31. Such reproof must include encouragement and help. Ministry is hard. Failures are to be expected—acknowledged, forgiven, forgotten, and avoided. Everyone needs help in this task. Part of the help is reproof; it is the "negative thinking" that can have powerful effect. Obviously, reproof is to be carried out conscientiously and responsibly (e.g., follow-up), and done in good order (e.g., following appropriate channels, confidentiality, etc.).

Chapter 8

1. Matt. 10:8c–10, RSV; cf. Luke 10:1–7. See Martin Franzmann, *Follow Me* (St. Louis: Concordia, 1961) pp. 85–86, and H. N. Ridderbos, *Matthew,* trans. Ray Togtman, Bible Students Commentary (Grand Rapids: Zondervan, 1987), pp. 198–99. Later, in a curious passage, Jesus suggested that they also acquire a "sword" (Luke 22:35–38). This is usually understood to mean: be spiritually equipped to face persecution.

2. For more passages, see Luther's Small Catechism, IX, 3, "Duties Christians Owe Their Teachers and Pastors."

3. It may be that part of his purpose was to dissociate himself in their minds from the kind of traveling Hellenistic teachers of popular religion and philosophy who did wrongfully take financial advantage of their hearers.

4. Phil. 4:15–16. He refers to this also in 2 Cor. 11:8.

5. *The Word of the Lord Grows* (St. Louis: Concordia, 1961), p. 138.

6. As is often the case in Paul's letters, many of the epistle's key thoughts are expressed by Paul in the thanksgiving section of the epistolary form, which he regularly expands into a sort of exordium, that is, an introductory statement of major themes.

7. Phil. 1:12–14; but all is not harmonious in Rome, Phil. 1:15–18.

8. Perhaps there is not a better commentary on 2 Cor. 4:12; Philemon 12; and 1 Thess. 3:8 than this verse itself.

9. Paul had his "plans," yet he knew that "man proposes but God disposes." Many of his plans he was hindered from accomplishing; cf. Acts 16:6–7; 1 Thess. 2:18; Rom. 1:13; 15:22, 24. He did get to Rome, of course—as a prisoner. Whether he ever got to Spain is doubtful.

10. Every cent, therefore, given to the church should be liturgically presented and placed on the altar. It is a gift given to God; it is no longer ours. When we determine how to disburse it we are doing so as His agents and stewards, not as people deciding what to do with "our" money. It is also appropriate for the congregational treasurer to put a "thank you note" and Bible passage in every installment of the pastor's compensation.

SUGGESTIONS FOR FURTHER READING

Betz, Hans Dieter. *Galatians.* Hermeneia. Philadelphia: Fortress, 1979.

Caird, G. B. *The Language and Imagery of the Bible.* Philadelphia: Westminster, 1980.

De Boer, Willis Peter. *The Imitation of Paul.* Kampen: J. H. Kok, 1962.

Ebeling, G. *The Truth of the Gospel.* Trans. D. Green. Philadelphia: Fortress, 1985.

Franzmann, Martin. *Scripture and Interpretation.* Springfield: Concordia Seminary Print Shop, 1961.

————. *The Word of the Lord Grows.* St. Louis: Concordia, 1961.

Hulme, William E. *Your Pastor's Problems: A Guide for Ministers and Laymen.* Minneapolis: Augsburg, 1966.

Kruse, Colin. *New Testament Models for Ministry.* Nashville: Nelson, 1983.

Jewett, Robert. *The Thessalonian Correspondence.* Philadelphia: Fortress, 1986.

Lohmeyer, Ernst, *Die Briefe an die Philipper, an die Kolosser und an Philemon.* 13th ed. KEK IX. Göttingen: Vandenhoeck & Ruprecht, 1964.

Martin, Ralph. *Reconciliation: A Study of Paul's Theology.* New Foundations Theological Library. Atlanta: John Knox, 1981.

Neuhaus, Richard John. *Freedom for Ministry: A Critical Affirmation of the Church and Its Mission.* San Francisco: Harper & Row, 1979.

Rengstorf, K. H. *Apostolate and Ministry.* Trans. Paul D. Pahl. St. Louis: Concordia, 1969.

Schütz, J. H. *Paul and the Anatomy of Apostolic Authority.* Societas Novi Testamenti Studiorum Monograph 26. Cambridge: Cambridge University Press, 1975.